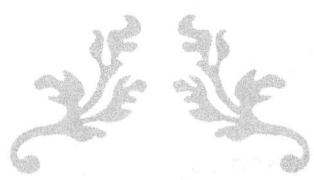

# 11 ASIAN MOVIES

Selected Masterworks from Asian Cinema

With 4 Bonus Movies & short summaries of 10 Asian cinema classics

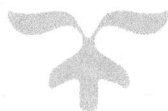

Copyright © Ugur Akinci | All Rights Reserved

# 11 Asian Films: Selected Masterworks from Asian Cinema

Copyright © Ugur Akinci | All Rights Reserved

ISBN No. B08GFX5L8D

**WARNING:** Some of the reviews contain sexually explicit or suggestive language due to the adult subject matter and story line of the movie.

**If you like this book, please consider leaving a review on Amazon to help us research and**

https://www.amazon.com/dp/B008EESE9S

**Many thanks in advance!**

# Contents

- Contents ............................................................................................................. 2
- Introduction ....................................................................................................... 4
- Raise the Red Lantern (1991) ........................................................................... 7
- Shanghai Triad (1995) ....................................................................................... 9
- Sweet Sex and Love (2003) ............................................................................. 11
- Woman is the Future of Man (2004) ............................................................. 20
- The Wayward Cloud (2005) ............................................................................ 25
- Stolen Life (2005) ............................................................................................ 29
- Isabella (2006) ................................................................................................. 33
- M (2006) .......................................................................................................... 38
- Maybe (2009) .................................................................................................. 43
- The Housemaid (2010) ................................................................................... 46

Parasite (2019) ............................................................................................................ 48

BONUS 1 — A Sun (2019) ........................................................................................... 51

BONUS 2 — Cities of Last Things (2018) ..................................................................... 55

BONUS 3 — Okja (2017) ............................................................................................. 59

BONUS 4 — Mother (2020) ........................................................................................ 64

10 Asian Film Classics ................................................................................................. 69

# Introduction

Here is an eclectic collection of new cinematic masterworks by exciting directors from China, Taiwan, South Korea, and Japan.

These of course are not an encyclopedic presentation of the countless great Asian films that graced our screens. It's a humble selection of those that I enjoyed watching during recent years.

**This edition includes 4 additional bonus movie reviews and short summaries of "10 Asian Film Classics."**

Every movie is presented with detailed plot line, selected dialog and scene description, followed by main plot points.

The collection starts with "**Sweet Sex and Love**" (2003), a South Korean film by Man-dae Bong (WARNING: explicit sex scenes).

Two lovers start their relationship on pure animalistic magnetism. They make love easily, frequently, with abandon, pretending nothing else matters.

But can they maintain their relationship purely through a bond that relies on frequent physical release?

This theme reminds us "No Strings Attached," a 2011 romantic comedy by Ivan Reitman, which explores a similar theme: the impossibility of keeping up a relationship for too long when it's based solely on physical sex. However, "Sweet Sex and Love" paints a similar story with a decidedly darker brush.

"**Woman is the Future of Man**" (2004) by Sang-soo Hong is the second South Korean film in this special collection that explores the following core dilemma: how to love a woman without betraying one's closest friend, a friend with whom the same woman carries out a relationship simultaneously.

How would one manage to pull off that kind of a relationship especially when one is married to yet another woman? A tough puzzle to crack.

"**The Wayward Cloud**" (2005) by the Taiwanese director Ming-liang Tsai is arguably one of the most experimental and audacious movies ever made (WARNING: explicit sex scenes).

In terms of sheer cinematographic imagination and creativity this is a work that rates 110 out of 100. It's an impossible-to-categorize meditation on urban alienation in which commercial pornography is presented as a pernicious stand-in and substitute for true love.

At the end of this film, you'll either love or hate watermelons but will definitely look at this fruit with different eyes.

**"Stolen Life"** (2005) from China by director Shaohong Li is a merciless drama about the indignities of belonging to a Chinese lower class.

The story is narrated through the viewpoint of a of a hapless and not-so-smart beauty from the countryside who gets used and abused without mercy in Beijing by an opportunistic heartbreaker.

It's a gritty urban tale about the kind of fate that sometimes awaits young girls migrating from the countryside to big sprawling metropolises like Beijing. Their hope for a better future is not always realized. Once they slip, there will be no end to their degradation and misfortune.

**"Isabella"** (2006) by Chinese director Ho-Cheung Pang is a story of redemption and a tour de force of sentimentality presented with stylistic authority where the soul-wrenching musical score (Portuguese Fado) emerges as the third main character. The other two characters are Chen-Shing Ma (played by Chapman To), a womanizer Macau cop under corruption investigation, and Bik-Yan Cheung (played by the luscious and luminous Isabella Leong), a girl searching for her missing father.

**"M"** (2006) from Japan by director Ryuic is another modern Asian masterpiece. A young house wife looks for the love and attention she thinks her husband owes her, but she searches for it in all the wrong places.

During her search, she gets tangled up with a pimp with underground connections. Only another and an unlikely character can save her. But the way he saves her opens up another chasm under her feet.

Despite all that, the director ushers the shocking possibility that some of the most important elements of the story might not be real at all. A great twist on a roaring story of betrayal and redemption.

**"Maybe"** (2009) is another must-see classic by South Korean director Jihong Ju. It's the story of an adopted Korean American woman arriving in Seoul to look for her real parents.

The taxi driver she meets at the airport will change her life in more ways than one.

When the cab driver's identity is revealed in the end, all the plot elements fall into place comfortably.

It's another classic story of redemption and wounds healed by making peace with the dreadful past.

However, at certain narration points, the audience has to assume that certain coincidences are indeed possible. Once such coincidences are accepted and attributed to "poetic license," the plot of the drama flows at its own organic pace.

The collection continues with an intimate look at the Academy Award winner South Korean masterpiece "**Parasite**" (2019) by Bong Joon-ho.

A class-war story as a dark comedy-thriller that won both the Palme d'Or and the Academy Award for Best Picture in 2020. Rarely do I see a movie that crosses genres boldly while delivering a social statement equally bold and uncompromising. It should be on your must-see list if it isn't already.

The four bonus reviews (**A Sun**, **Cities of Last Things**, **Okja**, **Mother**) in this expanded edition is followed by short summaries of 10 selected true classics of the Asian cinema.

Enjoy!

# Raise the Red Lantern (1991)

From CHINA.

**Raise the Red Lantern** is a stunning and emotionally powerful film that tells the story of a young woman named Songlian who becomes the fourth wife of a wealthy and influential Chinese man in the 1920s.

The film is set in a lavish mansion where each of the man's four wives is given their own separate quarters, and must compete for the attention of their husband by displaying red lanterns outside their door when he visits.

The film is visually stunning, with beautiful costumes and sets that transport the viewer to the opulent world of the Chinese aristocracy. The cinematography is also superb, with sweeping shots of the mansion and its lush gardens.

The acting is top-notch, with gorgeous Gong Li delivering a particularly standout performance as Songlian. She perfectly conveys the range of emotions that her character experiences, from hope and love to despair and resentment. The other actors also do a great job, particularly the actresses who play the other wives.

It's a must-see for fans of foreign cinema or anyone who enjoys a well-crafted, emotionally powerful film. A beautifully made movie that is sure to leave a lasting impression.

**ESTABLISHING SHOT:** 19 yr old Songlian, looking straight into the camera, agrees with her off-camera mother to be married against her will to a rich landowner.

**INCITING INCIDENT:** Songlian arrives in the walled compound of the rich landowner to be his Fourth Mistress.

**PLOT POINT 1:** Songlian realizes the Third Mistress will not give her a break and fight her nail and tooth for the attention of the Master while the Second Mistress could be a friend and an ally.

**MID POINT EVENT:** Songlian discovers in the room of her maid the "voodoo doll" used to put a curse on her. The maid admits that it was the Second Mistress who wrote Songlian's name on the doll.

**PLOT POINT 2:** The Third Mistress is murdered by the Master's servants "according to the rules" after the Second Mistress, acting on the information inadvertently blurted out by a drunk Songlian, catches the Third Mistress in bed with the house doctor who periodically visits the ladies.

**3rd ACT RESOLUTION:** Songlian goes mad, lighting the red lanterns in her apartment day and night while a young Fifth Mistress is ushered into the service of the Master.

## META DATA

- **Director:** Zhang Yimou
- **Producer:** Hou Hsiao-hsien
- **Writers:** Ni Zhen (Screenplay), Su Tong (Novel)
- **Starring:**
  Gong Li
  Cao Cuifen
  He Caifei
  Jin Shuyuan
  Kong Lin
  Ma Jingwu
  Zhao Qi
- **Released:** September 6, 2019
- **Run time: 125** minutes
- **Language:** Mandarin

# 🎭 Shanghai Triad (1995)

**Director:** Zhang Yimou.

**Writers:** Bi Feiyu (Screenplay), Li Xiao (Novel).

**Stars:** Gong Li, Li Baotian, Li Xuejian, Sun Chun, Wang Xiao Xiao.

**Shanghai Triad** is a crime drama set in the bustling and dangerous world of 1930s Shanghai.

The film follows the story of a young boy named Shuisheng who becomes the personal assistant to a powerful and ruthless gangster named Cousin. As Shuisheng becomes more entrenched in the criminal underworld, he witnesses firsthand the violence and corruption that permeates the city.

The film is visually stunning, with sweeping shots of the city and its many waterways. The sets and costumes are also well-done, effectively capturing the glamour and grittiness of Shanghai in the 1930s.

The acting is strong, with a standout performance from Li Baotian as Cousin. He perfectly conveys the character's charisma and menace, making him a formidable and unpredictable force. The young actor who plays Shuisheng, Zhang Fengyi, also does a great job, convincingly portraying the character's evolution from naive youth to a more cynical and world-weary young man.

This is a well-made and engrossing crime drama that offers a unique look at the criminal underworld of 1930s Shanghai. If you enjoy films in this genre, it is definitely worth checking it out.

**ESTABLISHING SHOT:** Country boy Shuisheng (Wang Xiaoxiao), just arrived in Shanghai, is standing in the midst of the urban crowd, totally clueless as to what's going on around him. A picture of confusion, alienation and anxiety. A fish out of water.

**INCITING INCIDENT:** Shuisheng witnesses a murder committed by the Tang mafia clan in the warehouse to which he is taken by his uncle.

**PLOT POINT 1:** Shuisheng witnesses the gorgeous Bijou (Gong Li), Tang's capricious mistress, make love to Sony, the boss's right hand man.

**MID POINT EVENT:** Shuisheng's uncle and the gang's several other members die during a rival gang's (Fat Yu) unsuccessful attempt on Tang's life. Tang retreats to a remote small island, taking both Bijou and Shuisheng with him and thinking of revenge. [Transition to a DIFFERENT WORLD.]

**PLOT POINT 2:** In a face to face confrontation, Tang reveals that he is fully aware of Sony's plans to assassinate him in the service of Fat Yu and the fact that Bijou slept with Sony.

**3rd ACT RESOLUTION:** Tang kills both Sony and Bijou, and takes Shuisheng back to Shanghai together with the small girl he met on the island to take Bijou's place in the future.

(Ends with) ...sound of water, choppy waves lapping against Tang's boat...

## META DATA

- **Director:** Zhang Yimou
- **Producers:**
  Yves Marmion
  Jean-Louis Piel
  Wu Yigong
- **Writer:** Bi Feiyu
- **Starring:**
  Gong Li
  Li Baotian
  Li Xuejian
  Sun Chun
  Wang Xiaoxiao
- **Released:** May 1995
- **Run time:** 103 minutes
- **Language:** Mandarin

# Sweet Sex and Love (2003)

From SOUTH KOREA.

## The Story

Shin-a is a young and gorgeous woman who obviously loves sex but is tired of the lackluster way her lover Gil Ki-hyun makes love to her. She's ready for a change.

She meets Dong-ki at a restaurant. They drink alcohol while they eat and get drunk. That leads to a night of explosive mind-blowing sex in very position described in Kama Sutra.

A few days later Dong-ki calls her and keeps up the relationship. He rides in a motorcycle right next to her van, serenading her over the cell phone until a cop pulls him over.

This is followed by another of the many sex scenes in this soft-porno flick in which she scares him by joking that he now has to marry her.

Despite all the surface physicality, Shin-a is growing a personal interest in Dong-ki, who is a nurse at a hospital taken care of a sick old man. She visits Dong-ki at the hospital and goes through his appointment book without his knowledge. Than he surprises him in the hospital's rest room. More kissing, groping, hands in each other's pants follow. They giggle like two kids doing it for the first time.

Shin-a moves in with him as he helps her carry many boxes of books. All that sweating and physical activity is of course followed by yet another quick-intercourse. This is a very joyful one, with a lot of fake protests, laughing and screaming and mock wrestling. Both actors are gorgeous; so we watch it once again without much protest. Sex, after all, seems to be core subject of this film.

CUT TO: They ride a motorcycle together at night, with Shin-a at the driver's seat, an adrenaline whipping ride against the traffic with an amateur rider at the helm. Followed by (CUT TO) licking chocolate off of each other's naked bodies and more childish love-games. They are still happy and laughing at every excuse. The world is good place indeed to breath and make love at every opportunity.

We watch the two grown-up "teenagers" grope their way through a few more frolicking episodes as they both discover one another and the city they live in.

In one crucial scene, Shin-a bumps into the Gil Ki-hyun and she has no choice but introduce Dong-ki to him. Yet she is at a lost as to how exactly she should define her relationship to Dong-ki. She ends up saying he is a "friend" while we know that's not quite true. The sense of unease and the tension in that encounter is the first sign in the story that things cannot go as is. The carnal (almost pornographic) status quo established between these two healthy gorgeous character is untenable; it cannot go as is and the story has to tip in one direction or another. That development comes in the very next "public restroom" episode.

Seeking to add some spice to their sexual adventures, the two lovers take it to a public rest room and try to get it on in a tiny stall. Yet a voyeur sneaks in to the next stall and takes a peek at them while they are deep into the fact. Scared and flustered, they leave the rest room in a hurry. What happened? They ask one another. Why didn't it this time went smoothly and ended up in shooting fireworks? What they don't know is this is the first of other downhill sexual encounters they will have in the second act of the story. This is the beginning of the unraveling and dissolution of their relationship. In the third act we'll see how the very physicality that once made them so blissful will fade away and leave its sad echo behind as a distant memory that's' impossible to recover.

"What are you ashamed of?" he asks incredulously, outside the rest room.

"This is a public rest room and I said I am sorry, didn't I?" she counters. The magic spell is broken.

STYLICTIC DETAIL: The main sequences in this film are demarked with "aphorism cards", black screens with printed "wise sayings" of unknown origin, such as: "Apologize with a penis and forgiven with an orgasm." It's hard to understand what to make of these crass "cards", a carryover from the era of silent movies.

Dong-ki at hospital. His patient experiences a cardiac arrest. Dong-ki is in absolute panic. He does everything to save the patient and eventually the patient is stabilized. CUT TO: Shin-a the seamstress is working at her tailor shop. She calls Dong-ki. No answer. She gets despondent and downcast. Goes back home unhappy. Back at the hospital, Dong-ki has a run-in with the insensitive male relative of the deceased. The bossy relative holds loud and inconsiderate conversations over his cell phone right next to the dying old man ("No, he won't make it tonight") while Dong-ki gazes livingly at the old man's eyes. Then the heart monitor goes flat and the old man dies. Dong-ki cannot hold back his tears.

On the way down, Dong-ki rides the elevator with the insensitive relatives of the deceased, including the same bossy male who keeps running his mouth on his cell phone: "The funeral is for 3 days... Well, he lived long enough...Hello?.. Hello?... Hello?... Yes, I'm in the elevator.."

NEXT: the doors of the elevator open and Dong-ki tumbles out, his hands around the throat of the cell-phone guy: "You call yourself a son?!"

"You fucking lunatic!" the man responds and two alpha-males hit the floor, exchanging punches.

Back at home, NEXT MORNING: Dong-ki wakes up late. He opens the freezer and finds a pair of frozen underpants that Shin-a made and prepared as a prelude to yet another round of sexual frolics. But this time he's not interested. He turns her a cold shoulder.

"No way I'm wearing these!"

Shin-a is deflated and upset. She didn't expect such an open rebuff from him. It's a first. She throws the underpants into garbage.

"You're unbelievable," he suggests.

"What? I'm unbelievable!?"

"My patient died last night. Do you know what I feel?"

Were they supposed to know how the other felt? Wasn't copulating like rabbits enough? Apparently not.

"Why didn't you tell me?" she shoots back indignantly.

"When did I have time? I just got up!" They already sound like long-married couples.

"You could've called me!" she shouts back. "How am I supposed to know if you keep it to yourself? You made me feel horrible!" This coming after many days and weeks of breathless pedal-to-the-metal love making at every silly opportunity.

"I'm sorry, okay?" Dong-ki backpedals. "So lets' just drop it." The water kettle on the burner has boiled and lets out a strong column of whistling steam – the perfect visual metaphor for the current status of their relationship.

CUT TO: After a shower, she gets up from her makeup table and curls right next to Dong-ki on bed and he spoons her. For the first time he touches and covers her in a gesture of protection and concerns that faintly smells of compassion.

"Wanna do it?" she asks, he hand already busy inside his sweat pants. She pulls down her panties. The "moment of compassion" is already gone and the two are back at their desperate carnal best. Sex is like a shorthand that they know too well. That's the only habit they can resort to whenever they find themselves in emotional turmoil. They consummate the act, as usual, but the earlier joy and mirth is gone.

The APHORISM CARD reads: "His fingers in my ass." Really? Why there is a need for such a vulgar statement at this point in the narrative, we have no idea. None of these cards makes any sense at all.

CUT TO: Shin-a at dinner with her friends, including Gil Ki-hyun who is going to get married soon and does not like to reminded of the fact since he still has the hots for Shin-a. She rubs it in by stressing the dull nature of making love to the same person all throughout one's life, reminding Gil Ki-hyun what's ahead for him even though he bores her.

Back at home, our main characters are again in bed, licking each other's selected body parts.

> "You've changed" she says. In response Dong-ki reveals either his tongue-in-cheek humor or denseness:
>
> "I haven't put on weight."
>
> "Not your body."
>
> "Look at me. You've changed."
>
> "Food goes bad, not me." The licking sucking and kissing continues and leads to another missionary-position engagement. But surprise! This time she has to remind him to go slow.
>
> "It's not all about you," she reminds him.
>
> Then he gets up: "Give me head."
>
> "Just do it," she suggests, mouthing the Nike slogan.
>
> "I'm kind of tired" he says.
>
> "If you're tired, let's not."
>
> "But I want to."

So she proceeds to give him oral sex while he sits in a chair. They are not equal partners anymore. He receives a service from a service provider. The only reason it's not prostitution is because no money changes hands.

After a few minutes of fellatio, they get on all fours in doggie position.

"That's the wrong hole," she reminds him.

"Let's try it" he insists and they engage in painful anal sex (despite lubrication) for the first time in their relationship, marking another milestone of disengagement and alienation. We hear her screaming with pain for the first time and we know this relationship is not what it used to be. Things have changed remarkably, for the worse. It hurts so much he has to stop. Something is definitely broken in the relationship. It's a turning point. When he wants to watch her later on in the rest room, she closes the door on his face. Oops.

Another stupid APHORISM CARD follows: "A selfish ejaculation, the fishy taste of sperm in the mouth." Hello?

CUT TO: Shin-a goes to Seoul for business and invites Dong-ki along. They are a mismatch already. Dong-ki knows he has no business to be in Seoul and he eats his food too fast, as commented on by Shin-a. He feels like an appendage. He calls her to see when she'll be done since he's sick and tired of sitting on stairs and smoking cigarettes, waiting for her. He has to return since he has to be at the hospital in the morning. Both are miserable. She can hardly concentrate on what she is doing.

They board the passenger bus to go back home. In the back seat where they're sitting, she starts to fondle his crotch and he returns the gesture by fingering her surreptitiously but the guy behind them gets annoyed; he gets up and changes his seat. Like they did many times in the past, they try to have sex in public but it's a clumsy attempt that they can't bring off smoothly. She ends up giving him a choking blow job, not exactly proud of what she's done.

CUT TO, NEXT DAY: "No one treats me like he does. It seems like I'm begging for it, and when it does, I hate myself," Shin-a complains to a friend of hers in a luxurious rest room.

"Because you're too proud," her friend replies and asks: "Does he cheat on you?"

"No."

"What's the problem then?"

"If he doesn't cheat on me, nothing's wrong?" Shin-a asks incredulously.

CUT TO: Shin-a finds a wedding invitation from Gil Ki-hyun, her former lover. Her expression is wistful and thoughtful. Later that night in bed, she masturbates for the first time. She is now alone in bringing the pleasure that she seeks so desperately in life. She can't rely on Dong-ki anymore, not even for sex.

CUT TO: Dong-ki is commiserating with a friend of his on the roof of a building at sunset. His friends praises the merits of marriage and tells him to marry Shin-a if he loves her. But Dong-ki is not sure.

"I don't think I can change," Dong-ki admits. He says he cannot become the person Shin-a wants him to be. It's a complicated business, this thing people call marriage, and they both agree at least on that point.

CUT TO: Shin-a and Dong-ki in bed, with their backs turned to each other.

"Tell me, do you love me?" she asks without turning around.

"Yeah," Dong-ki responds perfunctorily, after a long wait.

CUT TO: Shin-a is drinking with Gil Ki-hyun at a bar. She asks him about his wedding preparations. "It's okay," he says, without an ounce of enthusiasm in his voice. He reminds her to slow down lest she gets drunk.

> "That's the whole point," she responds, "you drink to get drunk, right?"
>
> "Any problems with him?" he asks, referring to Dong-ki.
>
> "Who?" Is her answer.
>
> "The guy you're seeing."
>
> "The guy I'm seeing? I'm not seeing anyone."

This exchange is followed by a hotel scene of ferocious intercourse between Shin-a and Ki-hyun as if there's no tomorrow.

NEXT MORNING: Back at home, Dong-ki is none the wiser. He is tired and disoriented. SHe is sitting in another corner of the house. None is speaking. It feels like the end.

Stupid APHORISM CARD: "When his penis changes, he changes too."

THREE MONTHS LATER. Shin-a has moved out and sold her seamstress shop. She had a few blind dates that led nowhere. She thinks of Dong-ki but resists calling him: "I don't think I can love him more than I did," she reminisces in voiceover. "I can no longer endure moments when he looks he is bored with me."

Then one day Dong-ki calls Shin-a and tells her that he wants to meet her. While he is waiting for her, a tremendous downpour catches him off-guard. She arrives in her car and Dong-ki takes refuge in the passenger seat. He admits how much he missed her.

> "After you left, I waited for you," he says. Rain is pouring by the buckets outside the warmly lit safety of the car.
>
> "Why? You shouldn't have."
>
> "I thought you might come back."
>
> "I missed you a lot," he admits "Let's start all over."
>
> "No. We'd better not."

But then she gives in and climbs on his lap and gazes deep into his eyes. Takes his hands to her chest.

> "Remember this feeling?" she asks, as her hand drops to his crotch.
>
> He responds by collapsing on her and they begin to rock back and forth.
>
> "I wanna have you" he says.
>
> "We're too much alike," she responds.

CUT TO: We see sitting side by side in their own seats. The rain is still pouring. We're not sure if they had full intercourse or dropped the matter after realizing it would never work between them anymore.

"Then… Goodbye," Dong-ki says, steps out of the car and walks away in rain. She can only watch him disappear from her side view mirror.

LAST SHOT is a video recording of Shin-a, probably shot when they were hot and involved and in synch.

"I love you… with all my heart," she says to the camera, and the film ends. An accordion steps through a romantic Parisian tune as the end-credits roll in in black and white.

## *** PLOT POINTS ***

**ESTABLISHING SHOT:** Shin-a makes love to her lover Gil Ki-hyun but she already lost interest in him. Having sex with him is boring.

CUT TO: Shin-a meets Dong-ki at a restaurant. Afterwards they make explosive wild love. Dong-ki and Shin-a meet again and continue their sexual tryst like two kids – full of joy, fire, and good'old carnal fun.

**INCITING INCIDENT:** Shin-a dumps her old lover and moves in with Dong-ki. Then, out in the street, she meets Gil Ki-hyun while she is accompanied by Dong-ki. This scene actually arrives 30 minutes into the film but it's still an "inciting incident" in the sense that the awkward tension in the way she introduces two men to each other underlines the eventually untenable status of her relationship to Dong-ki. It's the first crack in her unquestioned carnal armor.

**PLOT POINT 1:** After making love like rabbits at every opportunity and enjoying it to the hilt, the two love birds start to search for "variety" as all relationships based solely on sex eventually start to get wrinkled and frayed at the edges. They attempt to screw at a public restroom stall but the magic dissipates instantly when a voyeur in the next stall takes a peep at what they're doing. For the first time in their relationship, disillusionment rears its ugly head.

**MID POINT EVENT:** Dong-ki is a nurse at the hospital. One day his old patient dies. When a relative of the deceased man talks dismissively and disrespectfully behind the old man, Dong-ki finds himself on top of him, punching him without mercy. The awareness of death is a wake-up call that enters the sex garden of two lovers like a serpent.

**PLOT POINT 2:** After several disappointing and painful episodes of copulation, Shin-a accepts the advances of her old lover who is just about to get married. They have an energetic but angry and desperate Pedal-to-the-Metal Olympic Intercourse which of course does not change anything for Shin-a. The magic is gone and she can't bring herself to admit that perhaps what she's really looking for is gentle, compassionate love.

**3rd ACT RESOLUTION:** Shin-a separates from Dong-ki. She quits her job as a seamstress and sets up her own fashion business. She goes out on blind dates which doesn't mean anything for her. AT the end, on a rainy day, she meets once again with Dong-ki in car. Dong-ki confesses how he could never forget her and how he always thought she would return to him. They make quick love in the car. Then we cut to the last scene in which Shin-a admits her love (presumably) to Dong-ki through the POV of a video camera. We don't exactly know what actually happened to the two but we can assume that they've learned that real happiness lies beyond physical pleasures of sex. There is more to leading balanced and happy lives and they've learned it by paying the cost.

## META DATA

- **Director:** Man-dae Bong
- **Writers:**
  Bong Man-dae
  Kwak Jeong-deok
  Lee Soo-nam
  Seo-hyeong Kim (Jo Shin-a)
  Seong-su Kim (Dong-ki)
- **Released:** June 27, 2003
- **Run time:** 90 minutes
- **Language:** Korean

# Woman is the Future of Man (2004)

From SOUTH KOREA.

When Martin Scorsese praises a film, you listen. This is one such drama from South Korea.

However, this soft adult drama of missed opportunities and after-the-fact blundered attempts to recover some modicum of dignity, develops and ends without any firm resolution of the core dilemma: how to love a woman without betraying one's closest friend with whom the same woman also carries a relationship – and how would one manage to pull that off especially when one is very married to another woman?

## In a Nutshell

**Woman is the Future of Man** is a thought-provoking and emotionally powerful film that explores the complexities of human relationships and the ways in which the past can influence the present.

The film follows the story of two college friends, Mun-ho and Hae-joon, who reunite after many years apart. Hyun is a successful filmmaker and Mun-ho is an unsuccessful professor. As they spend time together, they begin to reflect on their past experiences and the choices they have made, leading to a series of conversations and debates about love, sex, and the meaning of life.

The film is beautifully shot, with a strong emphasis on visual storytelling. The cinematography is excellent, capturing the mood and atmosphere of the film perfectly.

The acting is also strong, with strong performances from the two lead actors, Kim Tae-woo and Yu Ji-tae. They have a great chemistry together, and their characters' conversations and debates feel authentic and engaging.

In sum, this is a thought-provoking and emotionally powerful film that is sure to leave a lasting impression. If you enjoy introspective dramas that explore the complexities of human relationships, you should not miss it.

## The Story Line

The low-key story starts on a snowy day with Hyeon-gon, a young film school graduate from an American university, visits his well-off university art professor and old friend Mun-ho. The two friends decide to go to a restaurant, have a few drinks, and shoot the breeze for old times' sake.

As one glass of liquor follows another, sensitive spots and psychic wounds are revealed. With the aid of occasional flashbacks, we realize that when Hyeon-gon left for America years ago, he left behind a teary eyed girlfriend, Seon-hwa, who soon became Mun-ho's sex partner as well – without, however, Hyeon-gon's knowledge who never realizes the fact throughout the film.

At the restaurant, both men make an opportunity pass at the pretty waitress (while the other guy is visiting the rest room) and offer her a role in a movie (Hyeon-gon) and a chance to work as a nude model at the art department (Mun-ho). The waitress turns them both politely. We observe both men also gaze wistfully at a woman waiting for her pickup out on the snowy street. We can only imagine what these two womanizers must be thinking at the moment.

The two half-drunk friends stumble out of the restaurant. Hyeon-gon suggests they take a taxi to go to the hotel where Seon-hwa is running a bar. The hotel is in a nearby city and is not really close but at the end they take a cab to visit their old mutual friend/lover.

After work, Seon-hwa takes both men (her old flame Hyeon-gon and her secret lover Mun-ho who proved to be a disappointing and selfish lover in bed) back to her flat where they continue to eat and drink. They are joined by a woman (and her dog) who is Seon-hwa's next-door neighbor. As the amount of alcohol intake climbs, the censorship drops and old regrets and old wounds float to the surface. Seon-hwa has the courage to reveal how hurt she was when Hyeon-gon left for America and how she waited for him for years without any news from Hyeon-gon. In return, a blabbering and very drunk Hyeon-gon is taken by regret and remorse to the degree he asks Seon-hwa to burn his arm with his own cigarette. The neighbor woman, realizing that the situation is getting too personal among the other three, leaves voluntarily.

What happens next throws a new light on the relationship of these three characters, explaining why the film ends the way it does.

First, Mun-ho retires to the couch in the living room where they ate and drank a few minutes earlier. Then, after covering Mun-ho with a blanket and tucking him in as if her were his baby, the "compassionate" Seon-hwa takes Hyeon-gon by the hand and take him to the bedroom next door, closing the door behind her. There is no question they Hyeon-gon and Seon-hwa have sex in there, even though the camera does not show what goes on behind the walls.

CUT TO: It's early in the morning. Mun-ho woke up and sitting on the couch. Seon-hwa walks out of the bedroom and sits next to Mun-ho. After a few words of small talk, what happens next is a true shocker. All of a sudden, the selfish Mun-ho asks Seon-hwa to give him a blow job even though he knows how and where we's spent the night. But obviously he doesn't care. All he cares about is his physical pleasure at the moment, damned be the social significance of such an intimate act.

To make things even worse, Seon-hwa accepts the invitation without any resistance and proceeds to pull down his zipper and give him an instant blow job even though the curtains of the apartment are open and there are other houses and windows just across the narrow street. At that point whatever authenticity we've attributed to Seon-hwa earlier evaporates. This is clearly an individual without a rudder and who takes each moment as it comes, without any allegiance or sense of obligation to any of the male lead characters. Afterwards, Seon-hwa and Muh-ho retire to the other bedroom for yet another round of quickie, presumably.

When Hyeon-gon wakes up he is none the wiser. The trio have a breakfast and leave the house as if nothing has happened. This is not a trio with a string moral compass and principles, for sure.

On their way back, they walk through the university campus where a group of soccer-playing students recognize Professor Mun-ho and they invite him to join them for a round of eating and drinking after the soccer game. Flattered by their attention, especially that of a particular female student who insists he wear her red scarf, Mun-ho accepts the invitation. Hyeon-gon and Soen-hwa say they'd like to walk to a nearby spring to fill their flasks with fresh water. They promise to meet shortly at the soccer field and they part. The initial plan presumably is to join the students all together.

But when Hyeon-gon and Soen-hwa return, Mun-ho is gone. They'll never see him again.

Irritated by Soen-hwa disappointment at Mun-ho's disappearance, Hyeon-gon throws a fit and leaves her while screaming how hard it has been to come back to her again, presumably crushed under a keen sense of guilt and shame for neglecting her that bad for that long.

We next focus our attention to Mun-ho, who has a small altercation at the restaurant where he joins his students. When a male student challenges Mun-ho's authenticity, Mun-ho flares up and creates a scene. Afterwards, the same female student who earlier offered him a red scarf at the stadium, joins him as he walks back home. Her intent is clear, she wants to be with him even if that means having sex.

The art professor and his student, they check into a cheap seedy motel with dirty mattress and tiny ugly rooms. She offers to give him oral sex and he accepts without any compunction. There is a brief scare of sorts when the male student who confronted Mun-ho earlier at the drinking table stalks them to the hotel. He briefly stands in front the door room as the fellatio is in full swing on the other side. We wonder if things will escalate. But the student suffices by banging on the door a few times and then running away. Inside, Mun-ho and the female student are scared out of their wits. Mun-ho zips up and opens the door but there's nobody there.

Last scene: it's still snowing in big city. Late night. Neon lights. A lonely wind that swirls the snowflakes gently across the near-empty street. The female student leaves with a taxi cab, leaving Mun-ho behind. The selfish art professor, who doesn't mind receiving a blow job from a student that he met just hours earlier while his wife waits for him at his luxurious home, stands there under light snow all alone, hands in pocket, staring at the wet pavement, as if he has no place no to. A great last shot that summarizes the predicament of a selfish character who has lost his moral bearings quite some time ago.

### *** PLOT POINTS ***

**ESTABLISHING SHOT:** A snowy day. Hyeon-gon, who has just returned from America with a degree in film-making, visits his old friend Mun-ho, an untenured university art professor, at the front gate of Mun-ho's nice home within a garden.

**INCITING INCIDENT:** Hyeon-gon and Mun-ho eat and drink at a restaurant to reminisce the past. Then, they decide to go visit their old mutual friend and Hyeon-gon's ex-girlfriend Soen-hwa.

**PLOT POINT 1:** After closing down the bar that she operates at a hotel, Soen-hwa takes both men back to her flat to party.

**MID POINT EVENT:** On that night and during the following morning, Soen-hwa has sex with both Hyeon-gon and Mun-ho, without Hyeon-gon's knowledge but with full consent of Mun-ho.

**PLOT POINT 2:** Mun-ho parts with Hyeon-gon and Soen-hwa while they walk across the university's soccer field in order to attend a dinner party with his students from the university.

**3rd ACT RESOLUTION:** Hyeon-gon runs away, leaving an angry and disappointed Soen-hwa behind. Mun-ho has oral has with a female student at a cheap motel. After that short episode, she takes off in a taxi cab, leaving Mun-ho all alone out there on a street corner and the snow keeps falling.

## META DATA

- **Director:** Sang-soo Hong
- **Producers:**
  Lee Han-na
  Marin Karmitz
- **Writer:** Hong Sang-soo
- **Starring:**
  Yoo Ji-tae
  Kim Tae-woo
  Sung Hyun-ah
- **Released:** May 4, 2004
- **Run time:** 87 minutes
- **Language:** Korean

# The Wayward Cloud (2005)

From TAIWAN.

The third film in "Tsai trilogy" [as designated by this author] since the characters Hsiao-Kang and Shiang-chyi are in Tsai's two previous films as well: "What Time Is It There" and "The Skywalk Is Gone" (a short film). If you haven't seen these earlier, you might want to start watching them first before tackling the much-denser and harder "The Wayward Cloud."

## In a Nutshell

**The Wayward Cloud** is a unique and unconventional film that blends elements of musicals, romantic comedies, and (yes) pornography.

Set in a drought-stricken Taipei, the film follows the story of Hsiao-kang, a young man who works as a pornographic film actor, and Shiang-chyi, a woman he meets while working on a film.

The film is visually striking, with a vibrant and colorful style that is both playful and absurd. The musical numbers are particularly memorable, with catchy tunes and over-the-top choreography.

The acting is strong, with standout performances from the lead actors, Lee Kang-sheng and Chen Shiang-chyi. They have a natural chemistry together, and their characters' quirky and unconventional relationship is both amusing and endearing.

A quirky and unconventional film that is sure to divide audiences. Some will be put off by its explicit sexual content and unconventional structure, while others will find it to be a refreshing and memorable experience. If you are a fan of unconventional cinema, this is one film that's worth your time.

## The Story Line

The film opens up with a scene that looks as though it's straight from the surrealist classic "Eraserhead": a man, Hsiao-Kang, is shooting a porn film by making love to a porn star through the half-sliced red watermelon that she holds in between her knees. Right away you realize this: the images you'll see in this film will be like none other. In terms of sheer cinematographic imagination and outrageous creativity, this is a work that rates 110 out of 100.

Here are the general elements of this impossible-to-categorize meditation on urban alienation and commercial pornography as a pernicious stand-in for true love: there is a water shortage in

Taiwan. That's one background motif that runs throughout the movie. Everybody's hoarding water in plastic bottles, including Shiang-chyi. In every scene there is at least one plastic water jug or bottle.

The best alternative to water is watermelons, which Taiwan seems to grow plenty of. This is a movie that makes frequent use of watermelons in every sense of the word, including as sex props and objects. Red juices of the fruit becomes a metaphor for blood which both gives life and is also the last thing that flows when a human life is taken violently.

Hsiao-Kang is a professional porn actor and lives in the same dingy apartment complex as Shiang-chyi. They develop a halting relationship that meanders around the real unspoken core of the film: how to develop something that feels like love that would survive the insatiable no-man's-land that is the sex act.

The absence of dialog or musical score in most scenes makes this a stylistically rewarding exercise while forcing us to fill in the interpretative blanks according to our own temperament and our own degree of engagement with the predicament of the main characters. Watching it is an open-ended exercise in semantics.

The Wayward Cloud is a visually stunning symphony of two souls trapped inside the lonely pleasure of their nerve endings. The plot, whatever there is of it, takes place in a bleak and almost dystopian urban environment, in gray corridors that lead nowhere, cold and wet public restrooms, sparsely decorated apartments with no kids or pets, all awash in gray-metal-blue color-pallet of dissolution and despair. There is plenty of copulation (yes, not "sex" or "love" but just plain old copulation), fellatio, masturbation, and other sex acts with or without human involvement to underscore the tenor of the story: alienated urban dwellers trying to get somewhere and experience something (anything!) through pornography in a hot city wilting under a merciless drought.

Then comes half a dozen song-and-dance set pieces a la Broadway in full chromatic color, complete with dozens of extras dancing and singing corny Chinese songs of love and virtue while twirling (yes) watermelon umbrellas or wearing outrageous pink cone bras and chasing a man-clown in phallus outfit all around a public restroom.

These set pieces of extravaganza are introduced so suddenly, without any segue whatsoever, that the first reaction is "what's going on here?!" Yet the hypnotic virtuoso aesthetics commanded by Tsai in some of these out-of-the-blue operatic interjections is so powerful, we are mesmerized all the same; we're literally taken hostage with the sheer beauty of these interludes even though cognitively we can't connect them with anything else that we've watched up until that point. The singing diva accompanied by a group of spider dancers and a flame thrower in the background is one such set piece worthy of mentioning. It's art-for-art's sake, exuberant explosions sandwiched in between all the doom and gloom that precede and succeed them.

This is one of those films that you need to watch at least twice to get the nuances and metaphors clearly. The director's imagination has created many disturbing images that point at some of the core ideas in the story. Take the house key buried into the asphalt by the steam-roller of a road construction crew, for example. Shiang-chyi tries to salvage the key but her vulnerable naked feet in slim flip-flops are no match for the hot asphalt pouring crew's steel-tipped boots. She is powerless to rescue the "key" (to her happiness? Relationship with Hsiao-Kang?) from the merciless onslaught of a busy city life that never sleeps. In a later scene we see the same key firmly embedded into the hardened asphalt – a subliminally disturbing frame that is metaphorically revealing at the same time. A true touch of cinematic genius.

The last long sequence is the keystone that holds together the bridge of anti-redemption that our anti-hero protagonists cross through. It is the shocking but anticipated destination of their anti-character arcs. They surface gasping for fresh air only after they hit the very bottom of their wretched obsession with pornography.

This high-voltage sequence starts with Shiang-chyi discovering inside the apartment elevator the corpse of the porn starlet that we watch masturbate in an earlier scene. Once the corpse is carried to a room in one of the apartments, a filming crew with lights, mike, and a camera materializes out of nowhere. Hsiao-Kang is available to shoot another porn flick but with a difference – this time, his co-actor is not even alive! The film crew disrobe the corpse and the position her in different ways to allow Hsiao-Kang to copulate with her while the camera is running. In a grotesque necrophiliac porn ballet, Hsiao-Kang starts to screw the corpse while Shiang-chyi observes the proceedings from the other side of the wall, through a lattice window. We are watching a simulation and emulation of "love act" so ridiculously fatuous that one of the "partners" does not even have to be alive!

Shiang-chyi starts to emit sounds while watching the filming, sounds that were interpreted by at least one film critic as crying and sounds of pain but can also very easily be interpreted as the fabricated whimpering of an orgasm-at-a-distance.

As Hsiao-Kang quickens his rhythm on the dead woman and edges towards his pitiful ejaculation, he pulls out, jumps to the lattice window like a mad monkey and inserts his penis into Shiang-chyi's willing mouth, who welcomes him in one of the most disturbing scenes ever recorded in film history.

What did that last scene achieve? Are our anti-heroes still locked up in their private hells? Or that last desperate attempt to connect unlocked something in them that was not accessible to both? It's hard to say.

This is a work that raises more questions than it answers. Watch it at least to realize the kind of visual possibilities that films can open up before our eyes; the kind of infinite worlds that the standard and complacent Hollywood fare helped us forget decades ago. That's why this critic concludes, despite all its seedy shortcomings and destructive imagery, Tsai's work is so jarring that at one point it cannot help but become a liberating tsunami for our imagination, by default.

### *** PLOT POINTS ***

This is not a film with any traditional plot points. But perhaps we can roughly identify the following "act themes":

**ACT 1:** The porn movie star Hsiao-Kang flirts with Shiang-chyi, a woman who happens to live in the same cold and mirthless apartment complex.

**ACT 2:** Through colorful song-and-dance Broadway set pieces, we come to realize the better (and perhaps even "noble") sentiments and aspirations that might be lurking behind the futile attempts of our main characters to connect through copulation and pornography.

**ACT 3:** Hsiao-Kang has sex with a corpse while a camera crew films and helps him, all a part of his new porn flick. He saves the "money shot" for the woman that he presumably "loves", Shiang-chyi.

### META DATA

- **Director:** Ming-liang Tsai
- **Producer:** Bruno Pésery
- **Writer:** Ming-liang Tsai
- **Starring:**
  Lee Kang-sheng
  Chen Shiang-chyi
- **Released:** March 18, 2005
- **Run time:** 112 minutes
- **Language:** Mandarin

# Stolen Life (2005)

From CHINA.

**In a Nutshell**

A hard drama about indignities of the lower class in China through the eyes of a hapless and not-so-smart beauty from the countryside who gets used in Beijing without mercy by an opportunistic heartbreaker.

**The Story Line**

The film opens with little Yan'ni, played by Xun Zhou, a small elf-like girl, taken to a train station by her mother and turned over to her aunt and grandmother for her upbringing. Raised by the two women, Yan'ni is constantly disparaged and pushed around. Her presence is resented bitterly by the two sharp-tongued acerbic women. As a defense mechanism, Yan'ni refuses to talk and wears a black cap wherever she goes. Her refusal to communicate makes things worse for her: those around her take her dogged silence as a sign of her stupidity and intransigence.

Yan'ni grows into a young girl of college age when something truly momentous happens: she is accepted to college! In a country where college education is available only to the very best, it's a truly life-changing event.

Yet the changes in Yan'ni's life is not limited to her college acceptance. In Beijing, se also meets Muyu at a traffic altercation. Muyu is a shy and seemingly well-meaning young man who happens to wear exactly the same trademark black hat that became Yan'ni's unofficial uniform. That creates an instant identification between them.

Muyu is a truck driver and takes an immediate and kind interest to Yan'ni. He makes sure she is settled comfortably at her dorm and she has what she needs from clothing to alarm clock. It's the big brother Yan'ni never had. She is touched by Muyu's respectful but genuine warmth. Thus soon she also falls in love with him and despite his protests that she is too good for him, she decides to leave the dorm and move in with Muyu.

And what a move it is! Muyu is living at the deep basement of a catacomb-like building complex, the kind populated by an underground colony of small businessmen and underclass families living in every nook and cranny. This suffocating and dispiriting living arrangement is perhaps one of the most interesting aspects of this film, uncovering for us the dirty underbelly of hard-charging Chinese urban life that we don't see that often in news from the world's most populous country. It's a soul-grinding cocktail of poverty, urban squalor, filth and hopes-deferred, all pushed underground where no sunshine ever penetrates. Yan'ni knows this is a step down socioeconomically and not up, but she loves Muyu. And their one-room underground hovel still makes her happy since Muyu gives her the love that was previously withheld from her by everyone in her family.

Then comes another crucial plot point: Yan'ni gets pregnant. As her belly gets extended, Yan'ni has a decision to make. One alternative is to have an abortion since the university rules (strangely enough) does not allow a pregnant women continue to be a student. It seems like the college official (herself also pregnant) has made it her duty to inform Yan'ni's parents about her pregnancy if she does not "take care of the problem." Yan'ni's pregnancy is obviously a big problem in terms of her future at the university.

The other alternative is to drop out of college and give birth to her baby. Muyu has always maintained that he would stand by her and support both her and their baby, no matter what. Yan'ni believes in Muyu with blind faith and does not even inquiry closely about his family or what he actually does for a living. All she knows is sometimes he is gone for long periods and he explains those absence by being on the road in his truck delivering goods for various customers.

Yan'ni starts to work as a food vendor on the streets. Later on she finds a position as a shoe saleswoman at a local mall. She definitely gambles her future on Muyu's honesty and support.

Her baby is a healthy boy. Both mom and the baby are in good health. That's also when we see yet another major and cruel twist in the plot line: Muyu starts to act cold towards her and starts to talk about the need to find a solution to their extreme economic hardship. One solution is pretty obvious: to sell their baby to a rich couple who can't conceive their own child and are willing to pay dearly for the gift.

Yan'ni's fate is sealed with a few devastating discoveries. She finds out that Muyu is actually married to another woman with a child, just life herself. The other woman chases Yan'ni away with a butcher's knife. Muyu explains it away by saying he does not love the other woman, the child was forced upon him by her, and he is actually in the process of separating from her, etc. Yan'ni again naively choses to believe in him but she is also visited at the shoe store she's working by the "new wife" that Muyu apparently took for himself while still living with Yan'ni. Things don't look good. Obviously, Muyu is not who he presents himself to be. There is a dark and sinister side to him that we discover layer by layer as the drama unfolds towards its devastating end.

Despite her misgivings, Yan'ni is forced to sell her baby to an affluent couple that Muyu has found. Shortly after, Yan'ni finds the hidden receipts of many similar transactions that Muyu has engineered in the past. At long last she gets the picture: Muyu is actually in the business of getting naïve women like herself pregnant in order to sell their babies to the highest bidder! He is a baby merchant.

When confronted, Muyu drops all pretense and shows his ugly sneering other face. Yes, he admits to everything and openly challenges Yan'ni. Muyu insults Yan'ni for her stupidity and we as the audience know that that's actually true while still feeling very bad for our heroine Yan'ni.

Yan'ni leaves Muyu and manages to settle to a somewhat stable life as a shoe saleswoman. Even though this is far below the kind of life she could've had had she continued her studies and graduated from college but at least she at long last realized her mistake and extricated herself from Muyu's deadly and humiliating embrace.

At one point she even considers killing Muyu and buys a knife for the purpose. But when the actual moment of murder arrives, Muyu brazenly challenges her to do it and she realizes she is not a murderer and drops the knife.

Perhaps the most unsatisfactory part of the film is its very last scene in which Yan'ni breaks the ultimate cinematic taboo and addresses the camera directly – that is, she breaks through the invisible "fourth wall" and pulls us the audience into the story. And to do what? She pleads us to help her find the child that she gave away years ago for cash. This does make sense neither for her nor us: we know that she knows that we have no idea where her child is; and we also know that her talking to us does not make any sense since we are not an actor inside the movie. The film ends on that totally unsatisfying and illogical scene with no resolution whatsoever.

A gritty urban drama about the kind of fate that sometimes awaits young girls migrating from the country side to big cities like Beijing with hopes of a better future. Once they slip, there seems to be no stop to their degradation and misfortune.

### *** PLOT POINTS ***

**ESTABLISHING SHOT:** Yan'ni is abandoned by her parents and given to her aunt and grandmother for her upbringing.

**INCITING INCIDENT:** Yan'ni wins and admission to college in Beijing and then meets Muyu, a young man, a truck driver, who seems to have only good intentions towards Yan'ni.

**PLOT POINT 1:** Yan'ni gets pregnant from Muyu and, instead of having an abortion and continuing with her studies, decides to drop out of college and give birth to her baby.

**MID POINT EVENT:** Yan'ni discovers Muyu is already married to another woman and has another child from her.

**PLOT POINT 2:** Yan'ni is forced by Muyu to sell her baby to a rich couple who can't conceive children.

**3rd ACT RESOLUTION:** Yan'ni discovers who Muyu is – he's actually a "baby merchant". Even though she considers briefly murdering Muyu, she realizes she can't do it. She leaves Muyu who immediately takes up another young and unsuspecting woman for himself. Yan'ni manages to pull herself together as a shoe saleswoman while continuing to look for her adopted child. The film ends with her direct (and strange) appeal directly to us, the audience, to help her find her missing child.

## META DATA

- **Director:** Shaohong Li
- **Producers:**
  Gao Xiaoping
  Li Shaohong
  Li Xiaowan
  Tan Xiangjiang
- **Writer:** Liao Yimei
- **Starring:**
  Zhou Xun
  Wu Jun
- **Released:** Aoril 23, 2005
- **Run time:** 90 minutes
- **Language:** Mandarin

# 🎭 Isabella (2006)

From CHINA.

A story of redemption and a tour de force of sentimentality presented with stylistic authority where the heart-wrenching musical score (Portuguese Fado) is the third main character. The other two characters are Chen-Shing Ma (played by Chapman To), a womanizer Macau cop under corruption investigation, and Bik-Yan Cheung (played by the luscious and luminous Isabella Leong), a girl in search of her missing father.

## In a Nutshell

Isabella (2006) is a visually stunning and emotionally powerful film that tells the story of a young woman who is struggling to come to terms with the recent death of her mother. As she navigates the grief and loneliness of her loss, Isabella begins to uncover long-buried secrets about her family's past that threaten to shatter everything she thought she knew.

She perfectly conveys the character's emotional turmoil and inner turmoil, and her journey of self-discovery is both moving and relatable.

A powerful film for an adult audience that is sure to leave a lasting impression. Definitely not a film you want to watch with your family or if you need a story that will make you laugh while enjoying your popcorn.

## The Story Line

This Hong Kong film directed and written by Ho-Cheung Pang narrates a story that takes place during the last 6 months between the summer and winter 1999 before Macau is turned over to China after many centuries of Portuguese rule. Thus in the deep background we have the theme of Chinese-Portuguese tensions about to be resolved, with Fado's romantic tango beat setting the stage.

The stage is set with the pure-red opening sequence: a middle-age man, Shing, is pressing a young girl (Yan) against a wall at a noisy night club, trying to drag her to bed. It's steamy, noisy, with random desire pulsing through veins, all torpedoes are ready to fire and damned be the consequences! The girl gives in and next we see them in bed, naked, coming back to their senses after intercourse.

The first plot arrives when Yan drops the sledgehammer on Shing: "I am your daughter…"

That really crushes Shing, the lecher, who made it a lifelong habit to run after every moving skirt to vent off steam. Womanizing is his "recreation" but this latest revelation crushes him. "Why the hell did you go to bed with me!?" he wants to ask her. Yan is philosophical. What difference does it make for him? Isn't he the one who throws himself at one tryst after another? He had sex with so many women that he would bump into his own daughter sooner or later and he wouldn't even know the difference.

Despite that, we are still unsure and uneasy about Yan's motivation to have sex with her own father. A twist late in the third act will cast a slightly different light on the relationship without, however, absolving it totally.

Yan gives two practical reasons for her involvement with Shing: she was curious where he lived. She wanted to see his house.

Second: she needs $3,000 in order not to get kicked out of her apartment – which of course makes her a whore even though, Yan is such an innocent-looking pretty thing, we resist the conclusion.

At this point we are introduced to "Isabella", Yan's missing dog. The landlord put the dog out on the street when she couldn't pay her rent and this fact, more so than losing her apartment, causes Yan to flip out. Why? Because Isabella is not a regular dog. It was actually given to her by her late mother; thus, it forms a living link with Yan's past.

Losing Isabella would mean losing her mother all over again.

After searching for days, Yan actually finds Isabella and reclaims her. Yet her pet's symbolism, a symbol of longing for what's important in life (unconditional love and care), continues as a precious thread until the end of the film.

Shing's life takes a different and permanent tack from that revelation onward. The depravity in which he finds himself was the wakeup call he needed; it seems. On the one hand he keeps roughing up various suspects in his role as an undercover cop, breaking a lot of bottles on other peoples' heads (bashing heads with a bottle is one of the visual motifs in this film that is repeated throughout, with a lot of fake- glass wasted in the process). But the worm has turned in the apple and his conscience won't leave him alone.

He starts to remember Yan's mother in faded-color flashbacks. The mother is the invisible leg of the emotional triad that forms the heart of this redemption story.

The mother died a year earlier of lung cancer, Yan explains. Shing, busy with bashing heads and transferring his genes right away to any XX-chromosome carrier who crosses his path, of course had no idea.

Despite the terrible start of the relationship from a most unlikely start-line, the hooker and her client slowly but surely start to bond and explore each other.

There is healing for both parties in that process, a healing that requires the acknowledgement of the current status as a prerequisite.

Thus, after a night of father-daughter drinking, the two hit the empty streets of Macau in the dead of the night, Yan announcing at the top of her lung the asshole-status of her father with joy, and Shing shouting that he is indeed an asshole and is almost proud of it.

Actually, what he is proud of is the way his young daughter owns up to him and is determined to stay the course with him no matter where their relationship takes them.

They both have been down for so long, any path seems up and good to them by default.

This is the midpoint where Yan moves in with Shing, complete with her own set of door keys.

Yan meets with Shing's girlfriends and invents all kinds of stories by inserting herself into the equation as his real girlfriend, in order to push them away and clean up Shing's haphazard private life.

To become a new person, Shing needs to reorganize his life, take responsibility for it, and Yan is there to make sure this time around her father will steer along a positive arc of change.

What follows is a few more "bonding sequences" in which the long-lost father and daughter ride motorcycle together, climb on top of a beacon and in general try to make up for lost time.

Two important plot twists propel us to the finish-line of the story:

1) Shing receives a phone call from his wife's second husband, a tailor who lived with her for 16 years while Shing was gone and too taken with his head-bashing and womanizing stupor to pay any attention to his wife or daughter.

The second husband reveals that actually Yan is not his real daughter since that baby was aborted at the hospital! Yan, it turns out, is this man's daughter but her mother treated her like an aborted child all the same.

So technically Shing has not committed incest but still the impact of that impression weighs heavily on him and is the direct cause of his tremendous transformation. Sometimes we all need that kind of massive shock to our system to amend our ways.

2) Shing discloses to Yan his dangerous involvement in a smuggling case. He went to bed with mafia for cash and now he has to pay the consequences. More than moral scruples are involved here – he is the fall guy, the one who has to take the blame for the crime.

His first impulse is to run away to Thailand. Yan enthusiastically supports his decision and declares her undying loyalty to him – she's going to run away with him as well.

But Shing's redemptive process runs too deep. His conscience does not allow him to drag Yan down with him to an uncertain adventure. The life of a fugitive is not for Yan.

Thus, to Yan's initial dismay, he decides to come clean and turn himself in voluntarily. He is confident he's going to spend at most two years in the locker after which they can get together, father and daughter, and proceed with their new lives.

One of the final sequences of the film shows Shing shaving his trademark moustache and wisp of a goatee and giving a new meaning to the phrase "coming clean."

He puts on his three-piece suit and just at a moment in his life when he looks like a serious businessman and a good citizen, he turns himself in to the penitentiary.

However, we know that both Shing's and Yan's life is on an irrevocably upward path even though Yan cries her tears of separation into the fluffy fur of her beloved lapdog, Isabella.

### *** PLOT POINTS ***

**ESTABLISHING SHOT:** Shing, the undercover cop and relentless womanizer, and Yan, the young hooker, neck heavily against a wall at a Macau night club. Red hot sexual tension.

**INCITING INCIDENT:** Shing takes Yan to his apartment flat and they have sex.

**PLOT POINT 1:** The morning after, Yan drops the bomb: she is Shing's daughter. Shing is crushed with this thunderbolt out of nowhere.

**MID POINT EVENT:** Shing admits he's an asshole and starts on the path to redemption and self-discovery. Father and daughter bond rapidly, trying to make up for the lost time.

**PLOT POINT 2:** Shing's ex-wife's second husband informs Shing that Yan actually is not his daughter even though she was given birth by Shing's ex.

**3rd ACT RESOLUTION:** Shing is caught in a smuggling scandal. He is the fall guy. He is facing jail time. First, he plans to run away to Thailand. Then he changes his mind and turns himself in to pay his due to society and comes up clean completely. Yan will wait for him and then the two will continue their lives together, as a family unit that they both need so badly.

## META DATA

- **Director:** Ho-Cheung Pang
- **Writer:** Ho-Cheung Pang
- **Starring:**
  Chapman To (Chen-Shing Ma)
  Isabella Leong (Bik-Yan Cheung)
  Josie Ho
- **Released:** 2006
- **Language:** Mandarin

# 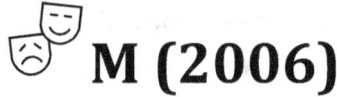 M (2006)

From JAPAN.

## The Story Line

A Mercedes Benz slows down to a stop at a red traffic light on a highway. Inside: a young man and a young woman behind the steering wheel. Both are wearing white bathroom robes. In voiceover, the woman says: "Why did he kill?... It was my fault too. Because I lied... though in truth I really liked Daddy Tatsuya. I said I liked Tetsu. So I'm an accomplice. It was me who made Tetsu kill Daddy Tatsuya and his mother." The rest of the movie is a long flashback of exposition which links up with this same opening scene at the very end of the film.

CUT TO: Young and beautiful Satako, a housewife with a son (Masato) and businessman husband (Hideyuki) going back home from a high school class reunion. In the backseat of the taxi, she is accompanied by Kodamo-kun an old school mate who makes an advance on her but she politely turns him down.

A telling detail that will become more significant at the end of the film: In the backseat of the taxi, Satako talks about Tetsu to her class mate ("he lived next door to me") but at first he does not recall Tetsu. She jogs his memory by revealing that they were all in junior high at the time. "You became much closer friends with Tetsu than I did and went to soccer games together." Then Kodamo-kun, who is obviously very interested to bed Satako than anything else, says "Oh, yeah, I remember now. What about him?" She responds: "Just wondered if you remembered; that's all."

Back at home and in her bedroom, she is taken aback by the fact that her husband Hideyuki would rather fall asleep right away than show any sexual interest in a gorgeous woman who strips in front of her eyes before curling next to him; this in spite of the fact that she reports to him how other men made a pass at her at the party and that "brought up old feelings" and made her heart pound faster. She is disappointed that he is not jealous at all. We can hear the worm of an ill-defined desire crunching its way through the apple of an otherwise "normal" marriage.

Giving in to stirrings of sexual hunger and morbid curiosity, Satako answers a cell-phone chat line and starts have affairs with men she meets online while also taking care of Masato.

A PARALLEL DEVELOPMENT: Minoru, a young motorcycle rider who works for a newspaper distribution company, makes his rounds around the city delivering the paper and collecting subscription fees while fighting his demons. There seems to be a volcano simmering below the surface of this taut young colt for reasons we don't understand yet. Then one day Minoru finds out that the beautiful woman at whose house he stopped by to collect the newspaper subscription fee and with whose son he played catch-baseball once in the past also happens to be same woman whose pornographic sadomasochistic photos are published on an Internet porn site.

Yet, dangers await at every turn in this risky path to cheap thrills.

Not long after, Jiro Tarawa, a Yakuza mafia member, posing as a regular customer, preys on Satako and forces her to work as her girl. Satako calls her pimp "Daddy". Daddy takes 30,000 of each 50,000 Yen she collects from her customers. At this point Satako is long past the point of no return. She starts to work as a professional prostitute who would do anything with a customer except S&M (sadomasochism) and anal intercourse.

Hideyuki also discovers his wife's secret life while looking at porn pictures on a CD provided by a colleague at work. The discovery changes his feelings for his wife altogether but he prefers not to confront her directly, perhaps out of his shame and the sheer shock of the unexpected revelation.

A major turning point in the story arrives when Minoru decides it's time to take the matters into his own hands.

Deciding to save Satako from a life of prostitution, Minoru breaks into Satako's house and reveals that he knows what she's doing on the side and he's there to "help". What follows are a couple expository flashbacks which reveal how Minoru has stabbed to death his drunk and abusive father when he was only a little boy and how Satako, when she was a little girl, took a tremendous liking to their neighbor "Daddy Tatsuya" and then dated his son Tetsu – until, that is, she learned the real reason of Tatsuya's interest in her family: he had a sexual relationship with Satako's mother. Minoru is pretty sure that Tatsuya raped Satako as well and that's why she needs to be punished by men that she calls "daddy". But Satako denies that and the possibility remains as an unproven hypothesis.

After meeting with Satako at a hotel room as a regular customer, Minoru ties up Satako like a hog and then forces her to call Jiro Tarawa, the Yakuza pimp, to come and save her. When Tarawa shows up, Minoru, who in earlier scenes has butchered up an old woman and the leader of the drug-gang with which he participated in the raid on the old woman's restaurant, stabs the pimp repeatedly and kills him in a very bloody scene. As both Minoru and Satako cry beyond control after the deed, she addresses Minoru as "Tetsu." "Forgive me Tetsu!" she cries out in genuine pain and remorse. So, is Tetsu a figment of her imagination or is Minoru really Tetsu?

The last two sequences brings this dark story to a tantalizing half-closure.

In the first sequence we hear Satako talk to her mother on the phone

## FIRST SEQUENCE

In the white Mercedes, as they escape the crime scene wrapped in identical white towel robes, both Minoru and Satako admit to each other that the stories they've told about their background were all made up. She did not go out with Tetsu, the son of Daddy Tatsuya. And Tetsu did not become jealous of her feelings for his father and Tetsu did not kill both Daddy Tatsuya and Mom and then set fire to his house. That admission makes Minoru laugh for the first time in the whole film. And the old woman that Minoru has stabbed to death in the raid, a woman whom he claimed was his real mother, was not her mother. "It was my father who I killed," Minoru says and we have little reason at this point to suspect that at least that part of the story is probably true. Earlier, we have seen the scar of a blade wound on Minoru's side that he caused himself by attempting at hara-kiri right after he stabbed his abusive father to death in their kitchen while his mother watched in horror.

## SECOND SEQUENCE

Life goes back to normal for both Satako and Minoru. Minoru returns to his newspaper delivery routine. And Satako goes back to her happy family while still believing that she hurt "Tetso" but there was nothing much she could do about it. She still believes "it made me an accomplice" since "because of me, he killed Daddy Tatsuya and his Mom."

A very crucial PHONE CONVERSATION between Satako and her mom sheds further light to the multiple layers of self-deception that lies at the core of this convoluted story.

"Hello? Mom?"Satako says.

"Our neighbor Mr. Kaneko passed away last night," her mother responds. "He was nice to you when you were small, so I thought I'd better tell you."

"Right."

"He had liver cancer. Tetsu will come back. You'd better show up as well."

"Right..."

"Stop over at my place if you don't have a mourning dress; you can wear mine. Should be an hour before the 6 p.m. wake."

"I got it. See you later then." And Satako hangs up.

So we now know that there definitely was a Tetsu but not quite what Satako made him up to be. And as to "Daddy Tatsuya", again, Satako's fertile imagination had a lot more to do with it than the real Mr. Kaneko.

The "truth" has probably been an equal mixture of facts and a dark imagination on the part of Minoru as well. Despite all the blood that's shed, the story leaves us with an odd sense of inexplicable "redemption" with both main characters going back to their regular normal lives.

### *** PLOT POINTS ***

**ESTABLISHING SHOT:** A man and woman in a Mercedes Benz that comes to a halt at a red traffic light in open country.

**INCITING INCIDENT:** Satako, our female protagonist and anti-hero, answers a cell-phone chat line and starts have affairs with men she meets online.

**PLOT POINT 1:** Jiro Tarawa, a Yakuza mafia member, posing as a regular customer, preys on Satako and forces her to work as her girl.

**MID POINT EVENT:** Hideyuki, Satako's well-meaning husband, discovers his wife's secret life while looking at porn pictures on a CD provided by a colleague at work.

**PLOT POINT 2:** Deciding to save Satako from a life of prostitution, Minoru takes matters into his own hands. He breaks into Satako's house and reveals that he knows what she's doing on the side and he's there to "help".

**3rd ACT RESOLUTION:** Minoru kills Tarawa the pimp. Minoru and Satako run away from the crime scene with a Mercedes Benz (linking up with the establishing shot). Yet we realize after a series of revelations that the "truth" has probably been an equal mixture of facts and a dark imagination on the part of both Minoru and Satako.

## META DATA

- **Director:** Ryuichi Hiroki.
- **Writers:** Seishu Hase (novel), Hisashi Saito (adaptation).
- **Stars:** Miwon (Satako), Kengo Kôra (Minoru) and Nao Ohmori (Hideyuki).

# 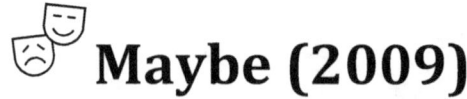 Maybe (2009)

(Alternative title: Lizard and Rabbit)

From SOUTH KOREA.

## The Story Line

Incheon International Airport, Seoul, South Korea. May, a 23 year old Korean-American woman, arrives from New York City after a long flight. This is the first time she's visiting the country of her birth since she was given away for adoption to an American family when she was too young to remember. She is now back to find her true biological parents. Even though she talks perfect Korean, she's a stranger in many ways in her native land. All she has in her hands to find her parents is an address scribbled on a piece of paper.

Outside the airport, taxi drivers are waiting for customers. And when of them is En Seol, a young man with an incurable heart condition. Once in a while his heart stops for 20 seconds. If it stops for another 3 or 5 seconds, he will die, as his doctor tells him. He is a guy who quit school after graduating from high school and gradually drifted towards the bottom rungs of the socioeconomic ladder. He is rapidly devolving into a loser as his friends marry, become high-earning professionals, and get on with life.

As May steps out from the airport, En Seol has another heart attack. He collapses next to his car in pain after showing his contempt for his doctor by putting a burning cigarette through his lung X-ray. But now he's in trouble. He can't breathe and is about to suffocate. At that instant he clutches at May as she is just passing by pulling her wheeled suitcase. He holds the lapel of her blouse tight and won't let her go. This is how May is introduced to En Seol per force. She has little choice in the matter, as fate would have it.

As we shall see later in in this story, this is just one of the several coincidences without which this story won't flow. But once you accept such instances as a matter of "poetic license," the plot flows in its own organic pace.

En Seol takes May to the address in her hand. It's an unassuming humble lower middle class house in a poor neighborhood of the city with narrow window streets. The house May finds turns out to belong to her aunt who gave May away for adoption when she was only three years old. Why was she given up for adoption? Because both her parents died in a traffic accident, her aunt informs her.

**\*\*\* PLOT POINTS \*\*\***

**ESTABLISHING SHOT:** Taxi cab driver En-seol drives through the night to a desolate building, which we later learn is an old train station. He tries get off the car to apologize (to somebody) but he is very sick. He collapses at the wheel.

**INCITING INCIDENT:** May, a 23 year old adopted Korean American woman, arrives at Incheon Airport, South Korea from New York City. Her goal is to find her biological parents. All she has for a lead is the address written on a piece of paper. Outside the airport, the cab driver En Seol is stricken down with his heart condition for which there is no cure. As he is convulsing on the ground he gets hold of May's arm. That how May is forcefully introduced to En Seol just minutes after she arrives in the country of her birth, decades later.

**PLOT POINT 1:** En Seol drives May to a lower-income neighborhood of Seoul. May finds her aunt at the given address. She learns from the aunt that her parents died at a traffic accident back in 1985 when she was three years old. The aunt put up May for adoption after her parents died since she, a dishwasher at a restaurant, couldn't take care of the little girl by herself. Later May will also learn another detail about her murky past: her father worked at the Yeseo Train Station.

**RUNNING MOTIF:** There is a motif that runs throughout the film. On May's back there is a wound shaped like a lizard. We never get to see the "lizard" but we know it's there and gets animated underneath her cloths when May is in a real distress. En Seol, on the other hand, is perpetually looking for a "red rabbit." He claims that if he finds the "red rabbit" he may just live a bit longer. This explains the alternate English title of the film, "Lizard and Rabbit."

**MID POINT EVENT:** After leaving her aunt's house, May has nowhere to go. After a long night of drinking, she returns to her hotel with En Seol but it's too late and the hotel owner locked the doors and went to sleep. She reluctantly accepts En Seol's offer to sleep at her house. May wakes up when En Seol has a nightmare about a traffic accident. When she wakes him up, En Seol hugs her with the embrace of a friend or a brother. That non-sexual embraces changes their relationship. En Seol is not a stalker anymore but more like May's friend away from home.

**PLOT POINT 2:** While going through May's belongings, En Seol learns the awful truth: he and May are actually siblings!

**3rd ACT RESOLUTION:** Through additional exposition we learn that May and En Seol were in the same bus as they were travelling with their parents. In the horrific crash, both their parents died while May got the deep wound on her back that looks like a "lizard." En Seol, on the other hand, witnessed an event that explains his obsession with the "red rabbit": his mother had a white rabbit in a cage she bought as a present "for my daughter." After the accident, the rabbit is seen hopping around, its fur turned red with the blood of the accident victims.

En Seol drives to the Yeseo Train Station to tell May about his discovery but he collapses soon after he makes it (which is the establishing shot in the beginning of the film).

Next morning, he recovers at the steering wheel. When he opens his eyes, May is holding his hand. They walk out to the train platform and bask in the warmth of their unexpected discovery. May arrived in Seoul to find her long-lost parents and she found her long-lost brother instead.

The last shot: a tiny white lizard on the train rail. It darts away and we symbolically realize that May is washed clean of the burden of the past, just like En Seol. Knowledge of the past releases the pain and depression that lurked for decades embedded in their systems. A rather Freudian resolution to a dramatic tear-jerker.

## META DATA

- **Director**: JOO Ji-hong
- **Producer**: Hou Hsiao-hsien
- **Writer**: JOO Ji-hong
- **Starring:**
  JANG Hyuk
  SUNG Yu-ri
  BAEK Hyun-ik
  AHN Seo-hyun
  LEE Seung-yeon
- **Released:** October 22, 2009
- **Language:** Korean

# The Housemaid (2010)

From SOUTH KOREA.

**ESTABLISHING SHOT:** Busy downtown Seoul. Bars and seafood restaurants district. Food is prepared and served all over the place. Throngs of people are enjoying themselves on a great evening. Our heroine Eun-yi Li, a young and beautiful girl, arrives at the scene riding a motorcycle with her lesbian lover. She is working at the same restaurant with her lover. Then, another young and beautiful girl jumps off from the top of the "B&B Bar" building and commits suicide, changing the whole mood suddenly.

**INCITING INCIDENT:** Eun-yi Li is hired to work as a maid and nanny at the house of billionaire businessman Hoon Goh. Goh catches Li while she is cleaning the bathtub, flashing her shapely legs from underneath her short work skirt. Goh is aroused by the unexpected encounter.

**PLOT POINT 1:** Goh enters Li's chamber with a bottle of wine and two glasses and makes love to her.

**MID POINT EVENT:** After another hot sex session, Goh gets Li pregnant while his wife is about to give birth to twins.

**PLOT POINT 2:** Realizing that Li is carrying Goh's child, Goh's wife Hae-ra poisons Li gradually. As a result, Li aborts and loses her baby. Li decides to take her revenge.

**3rd ACT RESOLUTION:** In a violently graphic last sequence that ends this dramatic story, Li takes her revenge in front of the whole Goh family in a way that would forever leave its mark on Goh's small daughter Nami, who always treated Li kindly and was aware of all the ugly and heartless relationships within the Goh household.

## META DATA

- **Director:** Sang-soo Im
- **Producer:** Jason Chae
- **Writer:** Sang-soo Im
- **Stars:**
  Do-yeon Jeon (as Eun-yi Li)
  Jung-Jae Lee (as Hoon Goh)
  Seo Woo (as Hae-ra)
  Yeo-Jong Yun (as Byung-sik)
  Seo-Hyeon Ahn (as Nami)
- **Released:** May 13, 2010
- **Running Time:** 107 minutes
- **Language:** Korean

# 🎭 Parasite (2019)

From SOUTH KOREA.

**A Class War Story as a Dark Comedy-Thriller that won both the Palme d'Or and the Academy Award for Best Picture in 2020.**

Rarely I see a movie that crosses genres boldly while delivering a social statement equally bold and uncompromising. South Korean director Bong Joon-ho's Academy Award winner for Best film Parasite is one such gem.

From the point of view of Joseph Campbell's "The Hero with a Thousand Faces" paradigm, this is the tale of a hero descending into the Underground but who can't make it back home.

The story of a poor lower-class South Korean Kim family which schemes and penetrates its way into the life of a high-flying filthy-rich one starts as a comedy and ends as a crushing tragedy with a lot of room for self-reflection.

Even though the film is in Korean with English subtitles, the narrative current and the visuals are so strong that it was easy for me to get swept along the story's dizzying eddies and waterfalls.

In its core, it's a simple story: A close-knit family of four (father, mother, son, and daughter) live in an arm-pit neighborhood of Seoul (a man habitually urinates in public right outside the window of their sub-ground level apartment).

I left the movie theater reeling, taking an internal survey of all the Kim and Park family members that I embody in one way or another.

Their apartment is falling apart; it's a trashcan with walls but they are street-smart, devoted to one another, and maintain a good sense of alert humor despite all the odds against it.

One day, just through the mercy of circumstances, the son manages to engineer his way into the graces of a super-rich Park family (who live in an architectural showcase of a castle) as an English tutor for their daughter. The story-rock that starts to roll down from that "inciting incident" point onward gains speed in every act and does not stop until it explodes in a terrific finale two hours later.

**SPOILER ALERT:** The Son makes sure his Sister, Mother and Father are also employed by the super-rich family as an art therapist, housemaid, and private chauffeur respectively without, however, disclosing that they are actually the members of the same family. Cheating on their credentials doesn't bother any of them until it's too late.

Body odor metamorphoses into an existential judgment with no exoneration as long as the income gap that characterizes modern South Korea widens.

While the "parasitic" Kim family is not a paragon of ethical behavior, the Parks are not beyond derision either. Especially Mrs. Park who is portrayed as a feather-brained and naive nouveau-rich housewife who has no clue what's going on in the world. Spoiled by her wealth and privilege, she is blinded to the predicament of the people whom she hires at a heartbeat, without any intelligent background checks, always motivated by her petty fears and trivial preoccupations that are laughable for the life-hardened Kim family.

Her husband Mr. Park comes across as less conceited and more grounded in mundane reality probably thanks to his role as the dashing and successful CEO of a high-tech company. However, he is also susceptible to the same class-blindness that in the end, like a worm eating up the apple from inside, brings the downfall of both families.

The tale of a "The Hero with a Thousand Faces" descending into the Underground but who can't make it back home...

The master storyteller Bong Joon-ho uses a very interesting device to drive the pain of class differentials home with unrelenting pressure: the sense of smell. When Kim's family learns that the Parks can detect a "curious smell" when the Kims are around them, that becomes a poisonous differentiator with unintended consequences.

The film's climactic last scenes are fueled with one last reference to the way poor people smell when they are around rich folks: an existential judgment with no exoneration as long as the income gap that characterizes modern South Korea widens.

Parasite, besides lush photography and good acting, also offers a second robust storyline: what happens in the mysterious underground bunker of the Park residence with its own horror-show of a history.

In a post-Oscar interview, Bong Joon-ho said the harsh contrast between the Kim and Park residences on the one hand, and the architectural showpiece of Park mansion versus its rough, semi-finished, and ill-lit concrete underground bunker, on the other, is his way of presenting the socioeconomic differences and class war in a "vertical arrangement." Architecture as a political metaphor could not be utilized more skillfully than this.

Parasite ends as it should: without a final resolution of the tectonic social forces that jumpstarted the story in the first act. I left the movie theater reeling, taking an internal survey of all the Kim and Park family members that I embody in one way or another.

An edge-of-the-seat thriller with plenty of opportunities to laugh out loud, followed by a somber acknowledgment of the powerful forces that both bind us and set us up against one another in our eternal search for power, pleasure, status, and money. What else can we ask for from a movie?

10 out of 10 stars. Highly recommended.

**META DATA**

- **Director:** Bong Joon-ho
- **Producers:**
  Kwak Sin-ae
  Moon Yang-kwon
  Bong Joon-ho
  Jang Young-hwan
- **Writer:** Bong Joon-ho
- **Starring:**
  Song Kang-ho
  Lee Sun-kyun
  Cho Yeo-jeong
  Choi Woo-shik
  Park So-dam
  Jang Hye-jin
- **Released:** May 2019
- **Running Time:** 132 minutes
- **Language:** Korean

# 🎭 BONUS 1 — A Sun (2019)

From Taiwan.

"A Sun" (2019) is the drama of a family of four from the Taiwanese director and screenwriter Chung Mong-hong.

The story starts with two guys riding a motorcycle in a punishing rainstorm in Taipei. They are Chen Jian-ho (A-Ho, played by Wu Chien-Ho) and his friend Radish, on their way to the kitchen of a restaurant.

## Graphic Violence You'll Remember

Before we can grasp the context and overall lines of the story, Radish and Ho ambush an unsuspecting group. Radish cuts off the hand of another teenager (Oden) with a machete before Ho can stop it. Ho taught they were just going to scare Oden.

The chopped hand falls into a boiling pot of soup — the kind of over-the-top but creative graphic violence scene that you'll more likely to see in a Chinese film than an American one. The image of a severed bloody hand sinking slowly into a pot of bubbling hot vegetable soup definitely stays with you whether you are ready for it or not.

## Wen the Disciplinarian

Cut to the trial scene. A-Ho's father Chen Yi-Wen, a mediocre driving instructor at a driving school, basically disowns Ho. When asked how many sons he has, Wen says one. Playing favorites between children never brought peace to any family.

## The Favorite Son

But he actually has another son, Ho's older brother A-Hao (played by Xu Guang-Han A.k.a. Greg Hsu), who is a tall handsome kid going to a preparatory school to win the entrance exam of the medical school.

For the assault, Ho takes on the blame and is sent for three years to a juvenile detention center and Radish sent to jail for a much longer term even though Ho lied by saying that he was the one who chopped Oden's hand off.

## A Mother's Quiet Suffering

Wen is proud of his older son Hao but as far as he is concerned, Ho deserves to go to jail to learn "his lesson." His wife Qin is up in arms against her husband's lack of support for Ho but there is little she can do about it except suffer quietly.

In Act 2 we witness how Ho manages to survive the hell of juvenile detention which looks more like Alcatraz than a "youth correctional facility." There is nothing corrected in there. The gang of teenagers don't hesitate a second to beat up the newcomers in order to protect the established pecking order in the house.

However, after beating up one such would-be bully to the brink of his life, Ho is left alone by the others until his release 18 months later.

## The Girlfriend

While Ho is still in jail, his mother Qin is visited by a young girl Xiao Yu and her "mother" who actually turns out be her aunt.

Xiao Yu is Ho's girlfriend, and she became pregnant before Ho went to jail.

Qin initially refuses to take any responsibility for his jailed son's yet-another fault. But actually, in an honest attempt to do the right thing, Qin takes the girl under her wing and allows her to move in with the family.

The news is eventually broken to Ho and the two marry in the detention center after their baby is born.

There are two recurring motifs in this long (over 2 hours) family drama.

## The Sun

The first one is the sun which gave its name to the title of the movie.

The sun represents life-giving light, truth, and goodness that shines equally on everybody and every animal on earth even though by the same act it also creates shadows where people take refuge to survive and to hide.

After getting released from jail, Ho starts to work as a car washer during the day and as a clerk at a convenience store at night.

## The Suicide

The major development at mid-point of the story is Hao's suicide for reasons not too clear.

In the morning of the day that Hao jumps from his apartment he shaves. I don't think people who are determined to take their lives shave first.

Secondly, up until that point everything seems to be going Hao's way. He is his parents' favorite boy, he has a romantic relationship with a nice girl, and is about to enter medical school. He is the sunlight of his family.

So why does he take his life? It's not clear. But the act definitely helps move the story forward.

His suicide forces a shocked Wen to switch gears and start to take his surviving son Ho more seriously. He becomes more protective and understanding of his younger son. This shift to a different stance will have unexpected and tragic results ahead.

## Carpe Diem

The second recurring theme is the slogan of the driving school where Wen works: "Seize the day — Decide your path," or the famous motto CARPE DIEM, as expressed in Latin.

However, at least in his wife's eyes, Wen himself seemed to have failed in seizing the day and carving out a richer and more consequential station for himself in life.

## Not Easy

Not all forms of "seizing the day" lead to positive results, apparently.

Hao seized the day and ended up committing suicide. However, it should be noted that the collection of "Seize the Day" annual planners that Wen gave as a gift every year to Hao is found in his room after his death — all blank. So perhaps he didn't find much in his life to record as proof of CARPE DIEM.

Ho also seized the day in his own way but ended up in jail after which he acquiesced to a life of insignificance as a car washer and store clerk pulling the graveyard shift.

When Radish shows up after a long stint in prison, he starts to make demands on Ho. As much as he tries to avoid a return to his previous life of crime, Ho ends up carrying a duffel bag full of money for the gang that Radish has close ties with.

## The Confession

Things come to a head on a rainy night when Ho makes another delivery but finds Radish murdered when he returns to his car. That seems to be the end of Ho's troubles or perhaps not. But one thing is clear: Radish won't be around pestering him with his demands anymore.

## How did that happen?

On a sunny day, after they climb up to a breezy mountain top with a sweeping view of Taipei, Wen admits to his wife that he is the one who followed Radish and Ho on that faithful evening and in a move to protect his son, he was the one who killed Radish as his son disappeared briefly to meet with the gangsters.

## 180-Degree Turn Around

The massive 180-degree turn in Wen's character arc is completed but the couple is now shaken with the facts of life and the high cost of doing the right thing. The father's love for his remaining son is absolute, touching, if a little too late.

The sun still shines but seizing the day still sounds like an empty slogan that fails to show individuals the right way to select the proper path in life.

An 8 out of 10 for this powerful drama.

## META DATA

- Director: Chung Mong-hong
- Producers: Yeh Ju-feng, Tseng Shao-chien
- Writers: Chung Mong-hong, Chang Yao-sheng
- Starring: Chen Yi-wen, Smantha Ko, Wu Chien-ho, Liu Kuan-ting
- Released: September 6, 2019
- Run time: 155 minutes
- Language: Taiwanese Mandarin, Taiwanese Hokkien

#  BONUS 2 — Cities of Last Things (2018)

Emotional outcomes stand in for causality in "Cities of Last Things (2018)" even when some dots don't connect through time.

When Quentin Tarantino played around with chronology in "Pulp Fiction," it was a novelty, a break away from traditional story telling which respected linear-time convention. Since then, many screenwriters and directors took his iconoclast lead and experimented with different versions of the same idea.

"The Curious Case of Benjamin Button (2008)," for example, directed by David Fincher, narrated the story of Mr. Button backwards in biological time. Fincher used a double time helix: the story time moved forward with us the audience while the main character's biographical time went backwards as he aged in reverse.

"Three Times (2005)" by the Taiwanese director Hou Hsiao-hsien took a different karmic path to time reversal. A man and a woman live the same romance in three different historical periods.

### Cities of Last Things (2018)

In "Cities of Last Things (2018)," the Taiwanese director Ho Wi-ding riffed on a different variation: the story of Zhang Dong Ling (played by a stone-faced Jack Kao), a man in his senior years, is narrated backwards to his childhood, through four different sub-stories, each corresponding to a different age backet: old age, middle age, teenage years, and finally, the toddler.

As a considerable number of Asian movies do, this one also opens with a scene of terrific violence: a man falls from the top of a high riser and splashes onto the pavement, with a sharp camera angle capturing all the gory details of a human body exploding on a solid surface.

At the moment it's not clear (like many other events in this movie) who the victim is but we are led to understand that he was Dong Ling, the main protagonist. He is a dour and humorless chain-smoking man in his sixties, with an intimidating masculinity about him, like a Taiwanese Humphrey Bogart.

What brought Dong Ling to his suicide is a number of disappointments and challenges that he always resolves or removes from his path with brute force.

## A Dangerous Bitter Man

The year is 2056 when people carry memory chips embedded into their bodies that cops can hook into and download the past events of a person's life.

When his disloyal and exhibitionist wife dances passionately in public with a guy who asks Dong Ling to divorce her because they are in love with one another, Dong Ling decks the guy and then strangles the woman.

He visits a prostitute (Ara) that he thinks he knows from somewhere, a possibility she denies.

Then we see him entering a hospital disguised as a doctor and kills one of the patients, the Minister of Health of Taiwan, but we don't know why.

Dong Ling's life is a series of seemingly-unconnected episodes of violence.

The police chase him for killing his wife but he shoots the drone that tried to capture him. He falls out the window ... Etcetera.

## Young Cop Against the System

The second (and chronologically earlier) phase of Dong Ling's life starts without a warning, as we watch him as a young cop at a police station.

He catches a younger Ara (who will become a prostitute later in life) as she is shoplifting candies from a convenience store. He acts leniently towards her and allows her to go free, earning her gratitude. That probably "explains" why he felt such a rapport with her in his future life as a much older man visiting Ara-the-hooker.

He walks in on his wife while she is having sex with his precinct boss in their very bedroom. He fights his boss who grabs his gun and threatens to kill Dong Ling unless he forgets what had happened and leaves the house. Dong Ling is overpowered. He has no choice but to swallow his pride, accept the insult, and do as he is told.

But he can't forget how he is humiliated. He is fuming inside like a volcano. It's a recurring nightmare.

To take his revenge, Dong Ling reveals the dirty secret of his fellow cops on the take.

As a response, they kidnap him and beat him up good. His boss tells him that, as he rots in jail, he will "take good care" of his wife. That's when we realize that we are watching this story backward since we have already watched the infidelity scene minutes earlier.

### Teenager Stumbles Upon His Mom

In the third episode, Dong Ling is a teenager caught for stealing a motorcycle. When he is chained to the same wall at the police station with an older woman, "Big Sister Wang," he is surprised that Wang knows a lot about his grandmother. Wang is there for refusing to become a police informant. She is caught after a long foot chase and brought to the station.

Dong Ling reluctantly realizes that Wang is actually his mother (what a coincidence?). He first tries to deny her but as they are led away in two different patrol cars, Wang is murdered at a traffic-stop ambush.

Perhaps that explains the traumatized non-smiling adult that Dong Ling is to become in his latter years. We sense a thread of continuity there between these different episodes even though there is no explicit exposition as would be in a classic who-dun-it flic.

### Sunshine of a Happy Toddler

The very last scene shows a much younger Big Sister Wang pushing a toddler Dong Ling on a swing set. He is such a lovely laughing good-natured little boy. It's a warm care-free mother-child relationship on a bright sunny day. They are both brimming with happiness without any inkling of the tragedies awaiting them both.

The story ends with that upbeat positive note.

### A New Viewing Experience

Even though the event chains do not segue smoothly and we are left scratching our heads how one thread of events led to the other through time, the director Ho Wi-ding perhaps tried to transport us, the audience, into a new viewing experience.

As Boyd Van Hoeij (a film writer based in Luxembourg and Paris) said in his authoritative Hollywood Reporter review:

"The director doesn't quite manage to connect all the dots across the three storylines... there are scenes that feel like they are more free-floating than they are organically attached to the rest of the narrative. But by the end of Cities of Last Things, there is absolutely a sense we have taken in an entire life, in all its emotional complexity and also with all its unexplained mysteries."

This is a seminal experiment of character revelation through reverse narration technique where some of the dots do not connect across temporal gaps. But we still get the emotional significance of a life unfolding both forward and backward. That's a high artistic accomplishment.

## Last Words

"Life can only be understood by looking backward; but it must be lived looking forward" — Soren Kierkegaard (1813–1855)

"Ne Oldum Dememeli. Ne Olacağım Demeli. [Don't worry about whom you had become. Worry about whom you will come to be in the future.]"

— Turkish proverb

An 8 out of 10.

## META DATA

- **Director:** Ho Wi Ding
- **Producers:**
  How Wi Ding
  Hyu Chi Hsin
- **Writer:** Ho Wi Ding
- **Starring:**
  Jack Kao
  Lee Hong-chi
  Hsieh Chang-Ying
  Louise Grinberg
- **Released:** September 8, 2018
- **Run time:** 107 minutes
- **Language:** Mandarin

# BONUS 3 — Okja (2017)

From South Korea.

When "Beauty and the Beast" Goes Vegan.
A genre-bending story from South Korea that may very well persuade you to quit eating meat.

A film by South Korean screenwriter, director, and producer **Bong Joon-ho** who, two years after this film, won an Academy Award for his urban class drama-black comedy thriller "**Parasite**" (2019).

Okja is a genre-bending story of many themes intertwined into a tragi-comic yarn. It's a modern take on the classic "Beauty and The Beast" theme, as well as being yet another story about the corporate evildoing in a capitalistic system where profits are more precious than human or animal lives.

Okja is at the same time a meditation on animal rights, what we do to them to satisfy our appetites, and the horrifying dark side of the meat industry.

It's the story of a little Korean girl Mija (played by Ahn Seo-hyun), who raises and befriends the super pig Okja, an elephant of a swine who is genetically modified by the ruthless Mirando Corporation to obtain more meat from pigs.

Okja is one of the 26 similar pigs that Mirando distributed to selected farmers in 26 countries and left there for ten years to see which one of these animals would be bred further as a new species of Super Pigs.

### Green Heaven

In the opening sequences of the film, we follow Mija and Okja in a heaven-like green mountain top in Korea with fresh clean air and sparkling rivers and waterfalls, frolicking and playing like two close friends despite the enormous difference in size between the huge animal (an FX miracle) and the little girl.

The animal is so big that Mija can enter his mouth with a toothbrush to clean his teeth. Even though Mija is living with her grandfather, she prefers to sleep at night under Okja, who, despite his enormous size, is gentle enough to cuddle her carefully and not harm her.

## A Sibling of a Pet

In one scene we follow how Okja almost sacrifices his life to save Mija from falling to her death from a cliff.

By all accounts, these two are more than two friends. Mija is not the "owner" of a pet. They are either siblings or lovers. Since there is not even the slightest hint of sexuality in their relationship, it's more apt to consider them siblings rather than "a pig" and "a girl."

## Turning Point

The "inciting incident" or the first plot point arrives with Dr. Johnny Wilcox (played by Jake Gyllenhaal who is cast in a role as far away as one can imagine from his usual leading-man dramatic roles), an attention seeking shameless zoologist, a spokesman and a shill for the Mirando Corporation.

Wilcox announces both good and bad news: Okja is selected the best of the cohort of Super Pigs delivered as piglets ten years ago to the loving care of Mija's family.

That's the good news.

The bad news is: the corporation wants to take Okja back to the New York City for a corporate publicity and promotional bonanza as a symbol of Mirando's solution to world hunger. Mija, as young as she is, is afraid that more will be done with and to Okja once he is in NYC.

They kidnap Okja one day when Mija is not at home. When she learns that Okja is gone with the blessings and complicity of her grandfather, she opens the rebel flag and runs after her beloved friend, running on foot at night from her mountain top to downtown Seoul.

## Go Mija Go!

In addition to breaking her piggy bank and grabbing all the loose change she could, she also takes with her a small pig statue made of pure gold that her grandfather gave to her earlier. This gold object, even though not exactly having the importance of a "MacGuffin" in a Hitchcock movie, would still turn out to be of critical importance in the story later on.

When Mija catches up with a tractor trailer taking Okja away, we are introduced to the ALF (Animal Liberation Front) activists led by Jay (played by the moody and enigmatic Paul Deno of "Little Miss Sunshine" (2006) and "There Will be Blood" (2007) fame).

ALF activists liberate Okja who runs through an underground shopping mall in a magnificent sequence of special effects. The FX technology used is so good and seamless throughout this film but especially in this scene that it's hard to believe we are watching a miracle of green-screen editing.

## The Betrayal

Eventually, Okja is taken to NYC thanks to a deliberate mistranslation from Korean to English (by a Korean ALF warrior no less) of Mija's desire to return Okja to the mountains. The evil Mirando corporation embraces Mija as the new face and goodwill ambassador of a corporation who needs a face-lift when reinventing itself as the solution to the hunger problem in the world.

Even though Mija initially plays nice with the hopes of taking Okja with her back to Korea when the NYC episode is over, she realizes that Okja is heading for the slaughterhouse once the welcoming party is over. The AFL activists manage to spoil Mirando Corporation's carefully choreographed parade through the streets of New York but they can't prevent Okja being taken to the slaughterhouse.

## The Horror

The third act exposes us to a horrifying picture of a slaughterhouse butchering this new species of genetically-modified super pigs who are kept in feeding lots surrounded by electric wire.

We are led to understand that these animals have families just like we do and watching their family members killed and cut to pieces before them only adds to their pain, suffering, and drama.

## "If it's cheap, they'll eat it…"

Towards the end, Lucy Mirando's dreaded twin sister Nancy takes over the reins of the family business (one of the many story lines in the movie) and pushes hard to butcher all new super pigs, including Okja, for a new brand of beef jerkies and sausages.

When her lieutenant Frank (played by Giancarlo Esposito of "Breaking Bad" fame who probably have never played a role badly) raises concerns about a public backlash, Nancy assures him that "if it's cheap, they'll eat it."

When Nancy, the bad ass capitalist, is asked why they have to kill these beautiful animals, her reply is ready: "We can only sell dead ones."

Mija manages to buy Okja's freedom from Nancy Mirando by exchanging his life for the gold statue her grandfather had given her. On the way out of the slaughter complex through a walkway surrounded on both sides by electric fence (with a strong resemblance to Nazi concentration camps), a super pig couple push their baby onto Mija's path to have their offspring saved. Okja hides the baby from the armed guards in his mouth and they are allowed to leave the premises while the ALF activists are sent to prison for sabotaging Mirando Corp.

## Back to Heaven

The last sequence: the colors lighten up from dark muddy gray of the slaughter house to bright primary colors of the same breezy mountain top back in South Korea. In addition to Okja, Mija and her grandfather now also have the baby super pig peacefully living in the same farm.

All is good. Violence has ended. Okja's life is saved. Ecological peace and balance is established. Mija and her grandfather are not vegetarians since they eat fish but an animal as intelligent as Okja is spared the fate of a creature way lower in the evolutionary hierarchy as a fish.

## Vanished at the Box Office

This film, which cost $50 million to make, brought back only $2 million at the box office.

Even though overall it's good entertainment, we are frequently asked to suspend our disbelief a bit too much as in the scene when the members of the ALF jump one by one from a speeding tractor trailer over the siding of a suspension bridge into the cold water below and survive the impact without a nose bleed. Please. Really?

Tilda Swinton, just like in another Bong Joon-ho film "The Snowpiercer," acts over-the-top in a caricature portrait of "the evil capitalist" and so does Jake Gyllenhaal who is totally miscast as a nerve-wreck zoologist who sold out his career to become a corporate shill. The fine actor that he is, I have no idea why he accepted this unremarkable role.

Ahn Seo-hyun, as Mija, was the real star of this film if you ask me. Her portrayal of an innocent little girl who'd do anything and everything to save her friend from mutilation and death is sweet and convincing.

I wish I saw "Paradise," a splendid story told with absolute authority of a director in full command of his powers, after watching Okja (which was shot two years earlier). But since I was already treated to the splendor of "Paradise" when I first watched Okja, disappointment was the inevitable normal outcome.

Chalk this one up as one of the weaker works of an otherwise very talented and accomplished director from South Korea. I give it a 6 out of 10.

However, Okja is probably the sweetest lumbering FX creature that you'll ever see even though it doesn't exist. For that, I'll add another point and bump my rating up to 7.

**The Last Word**

P.S. Do not quit watching when the end credits start to roll since if you're patient enough, there is a surprising little bonus at the end of the credits about what happens to the ALF warriors after they get out of jail.

**META DATA**

- **Director:** Bong Joon-ho
- **Producers:** Dede Gardner, Jeremy Kleiner
- **Writers:** Bong Joon-ho, Jon Ronson
- **Starring:**
  Tilda Swinton
  Paul Dano
  Ahn Seo-hyun
  Byun Hee-bong
  Steven Yeun
- **Released:** May 19, 2017 (Cannes Film Festival)
- **Run time:** 120 minutes
- **Language:** English, Korean

# BONUS 4 — Mother (2020)

From Japan.

What Would You Do if Your Mother Was a Monster?
Mother (2020) by Tatsushi Omori

Here is a film by the Japanese director Tatsushi Omori that is hard to watch but nevertheless opens our eyes to both the possibilities of realism in cinema and the unfathomable depth of the darkness lurking in the human soul. It's the kind of film that could've been written and shot by Michael Haneke, the great Austrian director of soul-crunching stories with no happy ending.

## Heart of Darkness

"Mother" is the story of Akiko (played with virtuosity by Masami Nagasawa), probably the worst abusing single mother you'll ever see in your life, and her maddeningly compliant son Shuhei (played by Sho Gunji (little boy) and by Daiken Okudaira (grownup teenager)).

Akiko's mental torturing of Shuhei is unrelenting, complete, and absolute. And so is Shuhei's uninterrupted obedience to Akiko's every command and whim.

She uses her own son to squeeze money out of her parents, sister, as well as complete strangers.

She prevents him from getting an education even when the opportunity arises.

She screams and hollers at Shuhei without warning for even the slightest excuse. Shuhei never sees those hits coming. The supposed "mother" uses him as her slave and servant to go find food to eat or steal something whenever the occasion arises.

Akiko even uses her little boy to blackmail grownup men with the threat of a pedophilia charge.

She does not hesitate to have sex at the drop of a hat with men that she wants to control or curry favors with, even when her little boy is right close by to witness all that uncontrolled lechery.

It's a relationship that would send any kid to a therapist lifelong but the enigmatic and vulnerable Shuhei hangs in there, twisting in the wind slowly, never having the courage to refuse what Akiko wants him to do.

## Roots of Resentment

The opening scene of the film provides some clues as to the reason why Akiko turned out to be such a monster.

Here we see Akiko accusing her parents of not paying for her university education while doing so for her sister. She has tremendous bitterness towards her parents and feels she is victimized by their favoritism.

In return, her sister claims Akiko could never have done well in college due to her laziness and bad grades, and thus justifies the reason why the parents had not spent equally on both sisters. Akiko's begging for money from her parents and their refusal is an ongoing thread in the story until the explosive tragic end.

## Enter Ryo...

What makes this picture of immorality even more fetid and rank is the character of Ryo (played by Sadao Abe), Akiko's equally abusive and immoral boyfriend of sorts.

Like two devils dancing in the flames of the same hell, Akiko and Ryo abuse Shuhei together without any compunction while running a step ahead from the law and the debt collectors.

For this tattered sorry picture of "a family," it's the most natural thing in the world to pick up their few backpacks and suitcases-on-wheels and flee in all hours of the day to another shelter or hovel until they exhaust their welcome there as well.

It's a life without any possessions to speak of, a haphazard life on the run, without a goal, aim, or plan, without any assessment of the past or desires for future. Living for Akiko and Ryo is but a constant drumbeat of getting something for nothing right here and now.

## The Last Disaster

In the last act of the film, Akiko asks Shuhei to kill her parents and steal their money.

Since the beginning of the story the family has grown into three when Akiko gave birth to a girl, the result of yet another thoughtless sex encounter with a stranger. When Akiko asks her teenage son to murder her parents, all three are homeless, wandering aimlessly along the streets and bridges of the city (Tokyo presumably).

Shuhei, who obeyed his mother's every other order, obeys this one as well.

He is caught and gets 12 years in prison when Akiko, again contrary to any normal motherly instinct, denies any involvement in the murder while Shuhei takes full blame. She shamelessly claims that Shuhei is known to lie from time to time and any hint of her involvement would be yet another fictitious claim by her no-good son. She is poisonous to the very end.

## Two Questions

There are two main questions that this film raises:

1) Why is Akiko the radioactive serpent that she is? How did she grow into this diabolic sociopath?

2) Why did Shuhei yield to every order and whim of a woman who is obviously a pathological disaster without a single redeeming feature?

Tatsushi Omori never answers the first question.

## Stockholm Syndrome?

The second question could be answered by the concept of "Stockholm Syndrome" which Wikipedia defines as "a theorized condition in which hostages develop a psychological bond with their captors during captivity... Emotional bonds may be formed between captors and captives, during intimate time together, but these are generally considered irrational in light of the danger or risk endured by the victims."

However, Omori's penultimate scene lays bare the roots of Shuhei's maddening (almost masochistic) passivity and compliance.

## The Crucial Scene

The scene is when Shuhei in jail, his long hair shorn and wearing the green jail overalls, is visited by Aya, a sympathetic social worker who herself was abused when she was a child and who wanted to save Shuhei earlier in the story from his hellish circumstances, without any success.

The dialog between Aya and Shuhei allows us for the first time to have a glimpse of what's going on inside Shuhei's heart and mind.

> Aya — Can I ask you something? I watched the trial. Why did you take all the blame? 12 years... is so long.
>
> Shuhei — It's better here than outside. I can eat regularly. I can read books.

Aya — Is that why?

Shuhei — (Turning his back to her to leave) May I go?

Aya — Wait! There's more, isn't there? Shuhei!

Shuhei — I love my mom.

Aya — Even now?

Shuhei — What should I have done? She is helpless on her own.

Aya — But you said you did it all by yourself. You shouldn't lie.

Shuhei — Why not? Everything about my life has been wrong anyway. But is it wrong to love my mother?

And with that, he exits the visitor's room.

Shuhei's life has been so full of horrific lies that loving his mother, despite all, emerged as the only truth available to him, or so he felt in the absence of any other yardstick of value in his young life.

## I (Must) Love, Therefore I Am

Just like the French philosopher Rene Descartes who decided that the reality of suspecting everything was the only thing he could not suspect, Shuhei also decided that loving his mother was the only measure of truth available to him, despite his mother's unmotherly duplicity and ferocity to the contrary.

His love for his mother is not a realistic transactional act based on good evidence but a philosophical one, a leap of faith based on desperation and self-preservation.

But loving someone also meant doing what's necessary for that love, or so he interpreted. And thus followed the murder, a crime planned and encouraged by Akiko but committed by Shuhei.

The film should've ended right there when Shuhei steps out of the visitor's room. But instead, it continues one more and needless scene of Aya visiting Akiko and telling her that her son said he loves her even when he is facing 12 years in jail. Akiko's response is a thousand-yard stare of an unrepentant and unredeemable sociopath for whom her son's misery doesn't mean a thing.

## Courageous, Disturbing, and Hard

A courageous, disturbing, and hard story, narrated with unblinking courage to lay bare a rarely visited corner of life on earth.

Gets 8 stars out of 10.

## META DATA

- **Director:** Tatsushi Omori
- **Producer:** Junko Sato
- **Writers:**
  Tatsushi Omori
  Takehiko Minato
- **Starring:**
  Masami Nagasawa
  Sadao Abe
  Daiken Okudaira
- **Released:** November 3, 2020
- **Run time:** 126 minutes
- **Language:** Japanese

#  10 Asian Film Classics

### 1) Rashomon (1950)

**Rashomon** is a 1950 Japanese drama film directed by **Akira Kurosawa**. It tells the story of a rape and murder from four different perspectives, each one contradicting the other. The film is renowned for its groundbreaking non-linear storytelling technique, which has since become a staple of modern cinema.

The film stars Toshiro Mifune, Machiko Kyō, Masayuki Mori, and Takashi Shimura. Rashomon won the Golden Lion at the Venice Film Festival and the Academy Honorary Award at the 24th Academy Awards.

### 2) Ran (1985)

**Ran** is a brilliantly crafted epic masterpiece from acclaimed Japanese director **Akira Kurosawa**. The story (taken from King Lear) follows Hidetora, an elderly warlord, who decides to abdicate his throne and divide his kingdom amongst his three sons. His decision to divide the kingdom causes chaos, resulting in a bloody conflict between his sons, and Hidetora's own descent into madness.

Kurosawa's filmmaking is unparalleled, creating an atmosphere of grandeur and epic scope. The visuals are breathtaking, and the cinematography is simply stunning. The performances by the cast are incredible, particularly by Tatsuya Nakadai as Hidetora, who gives an unforgettable and powerful performance.

Ran is a classic of world cinema, a beautiful and powerful film that is a must see for anyone who appreciates the art of filmmaking. It is a film that will stay with you long after it has ended, and is a testament to Kurosawa's brilliance. Highly recommended.

### 3) Spring, Summer, Fall, Winter… and Spring (2003)

**Spring, Summer, Fall, Winter… and Spring** is a South Korean film by **Kim Ki-duk**. It's an incredibly unique and beautiful South Korean film that follows a Buddhist monk and his young apprentice living in a small floating temple over the course of the five seasons of the year. The film offers a stunning visual journey with stunning cinematography, each season bringing its own story and themes to the table.

The movie is a thoughtful exploration of life, death and the cycle of nature, with powerful messages about how our past and present experiences shape us. The cast is excellent, particularly the young apprentice, who gives a heartbreakingly nuanced performance. The score is also superb, adding to the movie's ethereal, dream-like quality. Spring, Summer, Fall, Winter... and Spring is an unforgettable experience, and I highly recommend it to anyone who enjoys thought-provoking, visually stunning films.

## 4) Still Walking (2008)

**Still Walking** is a beautiful, emotionally stirring film from Japanese director **Hirokazu Koreeda**. This is a slow-paced, slice-of-life drama about a family gathering for an annual ritual for a deceased family member. The film is an intimate portrait of a family, and the many issues that plague them. The performances from the cast are all wonderful, creating characters that you truly care about. The cinematography is also very beautiful, creating a very peaceful, calming atmosphere.

It's a thoughtful, poignant film that really touches the heart — a quiet, subtle film that really speaks to the human condition, and will leave you feeling deeply moved.

## 5) Spring in a Small Town (1948)

**Spring in a Small Town** is an iconic Chinese film from the 1940s, directed by **Fei Mu** and considered to be one of the greatest films of all time. A classic masterpiece that Hong Kong Film Awards Association selected "the greatest Chinese film ever made" in 2005.

It tells the story of Liyan, a man living in a small Chinese town, and his wife Yuwen, who have been living in a loveless marriage for many years. Liyan is faced with the difficult decision of whether to rekindle his lost love with an old flame, or remain loyal to his wife.

This story is a masterful exploration of human emotion and the complexities of relationships, and it is wonderfully acted by the actors. The cinematography is also stunning, with scenes of the small town beautifully captured by Fei Mu's camera. The film has a strong, slow-paced rhythm that builds up the tension and emotion as the story plays out.

An emotionally powerful and visually stunning film that has stood the test of time and is still considered one of the greatest films ever made. It is an essential viewing experience that will reward viewers with an unforgettable experience. Highly recommended.

## 6) The Housemaid (1960)

**The Housemaid** is a classic South Korean film from 1960 that is an absolute must-see. The film follows a young woman who takes a job as a housemaid in an upper-class family. However, the family dynamic quickly changes as the housemaid slowly begins to take control of the household.

The Housemaid is a brilliant film that is brilliantly directed by **Kim Ki-young**. The attention to detail in the set design and cinematography is remarkable and creates an atmosphere that is both haunting and intriguing. The performances by the cast are also outstanding and each actor brings a unique and memorable quality to their role.

A powerful film that is both thought-provoking and captivating. It is a classic film that is sure to stay with you long after you've seen it. Put it on your must-see list.

## 7) A Better Tomorrow (1986)

**A Better Tomorrow** is a 1986 Hong Kong crime film directed by **John Woo** and starring Chow Yun-Fat, Ti Lung, Leslie Cheung and Waise Lee.

The film centers around a former Triad member, Mark "Gor" Lee, who attempts to lead a normal life, but is dragged back into the criminal underworld by his brother, Ho. The film follows their story as they struggle to survive in a world of crime and violence.

It is widely credited as the film that started the Hong Kong New Wave, and is considered one of the greatest action films of all time.

## 8) A City of Sadness (1989)

**A City of Sadness** is a drama film directed by Taiwanese filmmaker **Hou Hsiao-Hsien**.

Set in 1945 Taiwan, the film follows the Lin family, who are struggling to make sense of their past and present in a period of rapid political change.

The film highlights the traumatic consequences of Japan's 50-year occupation of Taiwan, which ended with the end of World War II, as well as the struggle of the Taiwanese people to come to terms with the country's new status as a part of the Republic of China. The film was the first to depict the White Terror Period in Taiwan, during which thousands of people were killed, arrested and tortured by the Kuomintang.

Through its use of handheld cameras, long takes, and minimal dialogue, City of Sadness creates a powerful atmosphere of sadness and loss.

The film was a commercial success and was a major influence in Taiwanese cinema. It won numerous awards, including the Golden Lion at the Venice Film Festival.

## 9) Harakiri (1962)

**Hara-Kiri** is a 1962 Japanese drama film directed by **Masaki Kobayashi**. It tells the story of a samurai who comes to a lord's palace to request the right to commit ritual suicide in the palace courtyard.

The film is a powerful exploration of the morality of honor and revenge that is as relevant today as it was in 1962. The performances of the cast are outstanding, and the direction of Masaki Kobayashi is masterful. The visuals are stunning, and the score by Toru Takemitsu is haunting.

This is a masterpiece of Japanese cinema and a must-see for any fan of world cinema.

## 10)     Seven Samurai (1954)

**Seven Samurai** is an absolute classic by Japanese director **Akira Kurosawa** that has stood the test of time and is widely considered to be one of the greatest films of all time.

The story follows a group of seven masterless samurai who band together to defend a small village from a band of ruthless bandits.

The characters are incredibly well-developed, the action sequences are thrilling and the cinematography is absolutely stunning. Akira Kurosawa's direction is exemplary and the film is a perfect example of his mastery of the craft.

Every frame of this film is a work of art and it is an absolute must-see for any film lover. Definitely recommended.

**If you like this book, please consider leaving a review on Amazon to help us research and write more books like this one:**

https://www.amazon.com/dp/B008EESE9S

**Many thanks in advance!**

www.ingramcontent.com/pod-product-compliance
Lightning Source LLC
Chambersburg PA
CBHW080521220526
45465CB00006B/2553